PRAISE FOR

The FIFTEEN Most Repeated *Lies* in *Business* Today

"This is a compact, well-written, and above all utterly *honest* book about how many in the senior echelons of the business world are prone to using cliches, half-truths, and ill-considered statements as gospel. Neil McNulty brings deep experience in both executive search and military leadership to sketch a better path: honest, defendable, and sometimes controversial communications that ultimately will shape a far better corporate workplace. A must read for leaders at every level."

—Admiral James Stavridis, US Navy (Ret); partner and vice chair of the Carlyle Group; chair of the Rockefeller Foundation; and former Supreme Allied Commander, NATO. Author of *The Restless Wave: a Novel of Love and War*.

The Fifteen Most Repeated Lies in Business Today will surely draw a variety of reactions from readers, and especially CEOs. Neil McNulty clearly points out the half-truths many CEOs and senior-level leaders echo in regard to such areas as remote working, subordinates evaluating supervisors, and "open door" communication companies, to name just three. He promises that readers will recognize all fifteen lies (I know I did) and also ensures each chapter ends on a high note by proposing solutions for effectively and truthfully addressing specific situations. A good read."

> —John R. Broderick, former president of Old Dominion University and author of over fifty published works on higher education.

"Neil McNulty has written an insightful book that captures the lies and half-truths leaders can tell others—and themselves—about their organization. He offers better ways to express in an honest and truthful manner that which can give leaders greater self-confidence and credibility. The author's long experience with organizational leadership and career development provides a superb background for understanding these leadership lessons."

> —General Anthony C. Zinni, US Marine Corps (Ret), former Commander-in-Chief, United States Central Command; special envoy to the Middle East; Fortune 500 CEO; and best-selling author.

"Neil McNulty understands the intersection between employee and employer extremely well. After decades of working with both parties, his book is extremely insightful. It provides guidance for both employers and employees to consider before final decisions are made. As a CEO (of a nationwide company), I appreciate that he points out how important it is to consider our answers to questions prospective employees will ask. Will our companies actually deliver on all that we promise? If not, perhaps it is time for us to make some changes."

—Mary Scott Nabers, President & CEO, Strategic Partnerships, Inc.

The Fifteen Most Repeated Lies in Business Today:
Falsehoods and Half-Truths Told by CEOs and Business Leaders
(And How to Rephrase Them)
by Neil P. McNulty

© Copyright 2024 Neil P. McNulty

979-8-88824-572-9

All rights reserved. No part of this publication may be reproduced, stored in a retrieval system, or transmitted in any form or by any means—electronic, mechanical, photocopy, recording, or any other—except for brief quotations in printed reviews, without the prior written permission of the author.

Published by

köehlerbooks™

3705 Shore Drive
Virginia Beach, VA 23455
800-435-4811
www.koehlerbooks.com

The FIFTEEN Most Repeated *Lies* in *Business* Today

Falsehoods and Half-Truths Told by CEOs and Business Leaders

(And How to Rephrase Them)

Neil P. McNulty

VIRGINIA BEACH
CAPE CHARLES

*Dedicated to my wife Mary Beth, son Neil,
and daughters Caroline and Kate.*

They always seek, share, and follow the truth.

TABLE OF CONTENTS

FOREWORD..i

HALF-TRUTH #1..1
HALF-TRUTH #2..7
HALF-TRUTH #3..14
HALF-TRUTH #4..20
HALF-TRUTH #5..28
HALF-TRUTH #6..35
HALF-TRUTH #7..48
HALF-TRUTH #8..55
HALF-TRUTH #9..63
HALF-TRUTH #10..70
HALF-TRUTH #11..77
HALF-TRUTH #12..84
HALF-TRUTH #13..89
HALF-TRUTH #14 95
HALF-TRUTH #15..101

THE TAKEAWAYS..107
ABOUT THE AUTHOR...109

FOREWORD

◆ ◆ ◆

What is truth?
—Pontius Pilate, AD 33

THE HUMAN CONDITION has always included telling lies and "half-truths" ("white lies").

Sadly, it is expected that almost everyone, no matter what station life, will at one time or another say whatever is needed to escape or avoid an unpleasant situation. It is the degree of seriousness which varies. Lies and falsehoods are so common that even in our courts of law, one must first take an oath to "tell the truth, and nothing but the truth" before testifying. The exception: the "George Washington" types who are believed to never lie about anything. In today's world, they are called extreme. Admission to chopping down a cherry tree is far less serious than admission to some of the things lied about in business today.

What is the difference between a lie and a half-truth? Frankly, the simplest definition of a lie is any known falsehood which is spoken, written, or advanced through an omission. For the purposes of this book, it can be defined as "a misleading or false statement or omission which causes some degree of harm." If there is no harm, for the purposes of this book, we will not call it a lie. Yes, that leaves out many lies.

Half-truths are a bit more complicated. They are truthful—sort of. Some are more harmful than others. And some half-truths are genuinely good. Examples of good half-truths include telling a host that the food they served was delicious while much of it was awful. Or being asked your opinion of a person's clothing which you say is beautiful, and you actually think it is less than flattering. Or being a fear-filled CEO in the middle of a serious business crisis yet speaking and acting confidently and in total command rather than being truthful and withdrawing into a shell (in other words—displaying true courage). In this book, we will use the words "lies" and "half-truths" interchangeably.

In business, most lies are harmful, and some are severely damaging, such as a CEO lying about a defective product which causes physical harm or advocating a stock which insiders know is about to crash. Big or small, lies in business cause harm and can even destroy an entire company and the lives of the people who work there. And when a Chief Executive Officer (CEO) tells a lie, it is more damaging than ever. That's because CEOs are generally assumed to be honest. Some aren't.

This book examines the most commonly repeated lies in business today, and these are often coming from the very highest levels of organizations: the C-suite and general managerial levels. Additionally, many of the lies have been repeated so often that they are now popular beliefs. A prime example is how many "experts" say remote and hybrid work is embraced by corporate America. The truth: when asked publicly, many executives will say they fully support remote work and believe it is the future. Privately, many of these same executives intensely dislike remote work and are actually planning an eventual return to offices by making working in a physical office the only way to get it done. In other words, they are not lying outright about remote work, but they are not supportive either.

As an executive search consultant since 1984, my tenure alone places me in the top 1 percent of my industry, and I have had confidential discussions with thousands of business leaders. At the risk of appearing less than humble, very few professionals have the trust-building skills required to get senior executives to open up to a near-stranger about some of the most sensitive details of their professional and personal lives. To succeed as an executive recruiter (yes, it's okay to call them "headhunters"), you need to be part sales representative, psychologist, and matchmaker (and probably a few more professions). Most importantly, you must be comfortable dealing on equal footing with stratospherically successful people, many with enormous egos, and not subordinate yourself or be intimidated by their success. Most can't, and they leave the business within a few years.

I have placed, coached, and counseled countless senior-level business leaders, all who shared their true beliefs with me. Without sharing those innermost true beliefs, which often contradict their public statements, they cannot be placed, because it would be impossible to make a match. This book reveals what many (not all, so do not be offended) secretly think about many of the biggest issues in business today. No confidences are violated, and I do not reveal names of individuals or companies. Some might claim that is a "cop out" or "bait and switch" based upon this book's title, and that is understandable. However, the purpose of this book is not to embarrass any individuals or companies (or get myself sued). Its purpose is to make things better for both business leaders and the people they lead.

The lies and half-truths discussed in this book are the ones most frequently heard coming from leaders of organizations, at organizations ranging in size from Fortune 500 to "mom and pop." The information is anecdotal—information I have personally received, and it is strictly my opinions. Additionally, it is very important to note that not all who say the fifteen statements are lying. Many senior business leaders are being sincere when they say them, but just as many of them know they are being less than truthful, and they are the focus of this book. In the end, you must be the judge of whether or not a business leader is being truthful.

If you have a career, you have heard all fifteen lies. If you are beginning your career, you will hear some of them soon, perhaps even in your first interview at a company. If that happens, do not reject a company simply because an interviewer repeated one or more of the falsehoods in this book. They might actually believe them and therefore aren't lying. Also, many of the lies begin as well-intentioned aspirations and are communicated truthfully as guiding principles. Employees feel optimistic, empowered, and excited. Then, over time, they realize those words are untrue, and what began as true aspirational goals often become unattainable due to changing realities. However, the problems arise when even with the changing realities, many organizations doggedly stick to the statements, knowing they are no longer true, which then makes them lies. Either way, team members feel conned.

In fact, you might actually tell the lies yourself,

and you may have repeated them so often they now seem unretractable without embarrassment or admitting you have been less than fully truthful. The good news is at the end of each chapter is a recommended rephrasing solution that is truthful yet preserves the original intent. Some might even add some new tools for you personally going forward to be truthful without appearing to have lied in the past.

What causes the lies?

Today, the lies usually can be traced to how organizations go to extraordinary lengths to be seen as customer-and-employee-focused, progressive, caring, and socially conscious. However, people who lead the organizations, those who deal with strategic level business realities, often know better. They know such burnished image-making is mostly untrue, a mirage, but to admit publicly what they truly believe could get them fired. But they do share their true feelings with executive search consultants. If they don't, they will be presented with career opportunities which perpetuate their dissatisfaction, or candidates for employment who are not a good fit. They need to level with us in order for us to make matches.

It's unfortunate the fifteen statements are often untrue because they are about truly good things. Organizations which sincerely aspire to many of from Fortune 500 to "mom and pop." The information is anecdotal—information I have personally received, and it is strictly my opinions. Additionally, it is very important to note that not all who say the fifteen statements are lying. Many senior business leaders are being sincere when they say them, but just as many of them know they are being less than truthful, and they are the focus of this book. In the end, you must be the judge of whether or not a business leader is being truthful.

If you have a career, you have heard all fifteen lies. If you are beginning your career, you will hear some of them soon, perhaps even in your first interview at a company. If that happens, do not reject a company simply because an interviewer repeated one or more of the falsehoods in this book. They might actually believe them and therefore aren't lying. Also, many of the lies begin as well-intentioned aspirations and are communicated truthfully as guiding principles. Employees feel optimistic, empowered, and excited. Then, over time, they realize those words are untrue, and what began as true aspirational goals often become unattainable due to changing realities. However, the problems arise when even with the changing realities, many organizations doggedly stick to the statements, knowing they are no longer true, which then makes them lies. Either way, team members feel conned.

In fact, you might actually tell the lies yourself,

and you may have repeated them so often they now seem unretractable without embarrassment or admitting you have been less than fully truthful. The good news is at the end of each chapter is a recommended rephrasing solution that is truthful yet preserves the original intent. Some might even add some new tools for you personally going forward to be truthful without appearing to have lied in the past.

What causes the lies?

Today, the lies usually can be traced to how organizations go to extraordinary lengths to be seen as customer-and-employee-focused, progressive, caring, and socially conscious. However, people who lead the organizations, those who deal with strategic level business realities, often know better. They know such burnished image-making is mostly untrue, a mirage, but to admit publicly what they truly believe could get them fired. But they do share their true feelings with executive search consultants. If they don't, they will be presented with career opportunities which perpetuate their dissatisfaction, or candidates for employment who are not a good fit. They need to level with us in order for us to make matches.

It's unfortunate the fifteen statements are often untrue because they are about truly good things. Organizations which sincerely aspire to many of them are genuinely great, but they are the exception—about 5 percent of American businesses. In my opinion, no companies actually abide by all of them, because they set almost impossible standards.

Many of the lies are also taught in business schools as hallmarks of great companies, often by professors who lack real-world business experience or who take a company's public statements at face value. Additionally, a review of the most recent speakers at major universities should confirm that many notable people are promoting the lies. They either do not know they are untrue, or they do know, but they are simply playing to popular themes to get great reviews (and more engagements).

Why are the statements untrue? The answer is simple: no matter how progressive an organization becomes, or how it advances new ideas and concepts, or how radically business changes, human nature does not change, and most of the lies defy human nature.

Placing high value on the needs and desires of employees and customers in business is a wonderful concept. Adopting personnel policies and changes that keep an organization up to date and a fun place to work seem critical in an era of razor-sharp talent acquisition competition. But human needs and desires remain a constant throughout every era. No doubt, business has changed radically over the millennia, since merchants first bartered. What has never changed is how Maslow's Hierarchy of Needs is just as applicable today as when it was first explained. That is, humans will say and do whatever it takes to protect or advance what is important to them, like their livelihood.

Because human nature never changes, there needs to be boundaries in every organization that never change. Unfortunately, the necessary boundaries are often viewed today as "stale," "old thinking," or "outdated." Many of the lies go directly against traditional boundaries. For example, no matter how egalitarian a company tries to project itself ("no bosses here"), someone needs to have the power to hire, fire, and control messaging. In fact, some of the most successful companies in history such as Procter & Gamble, PepsiCo, and General Electric have traditional leadership, formal chains of command, and protocols that do not change. They consistently thrive because even though many of their policies and procedures might change, the leaders at these companies know the difference between what can change and what should never change, no matter what the current trend is.

By defying traditional boundaries, it often results in the demise of previously successful companies. An excellent example of this was a biotech company in Virginia, known as one of the ten most successful startups in the Commonwealth since the year 2000.

The company was founded with discipline, strict protocols, and traditional leadership, due mostly to the scientific nature of its industry. However, once it achieved great success, the company shifted its recruitment efforts toward recent college graduates. It added youth-targeted perks such as offering days working from home each month (before COVID), flexible hours, on-site gym, health clinic, child-care, and a national franchise coffee bar with free coffee, stand-up desks, scooters, adult tricycles, and large bouncing balls in common areas, "bring your pet to work" days, and a cafeteria with free food at lunch. It also advertised an "open communication, flexible, and fun atmosphere" in recruiting materials. It became the "go to" employer for recent grads.

Eventually, reality happened. Employees were being well-paid for decreasing productivity and poor-quality work (too busy having fun). There were interruptions from pets (barking dogs, walking the pets, etc.), perks became too expensive to sustain or were abused (example: smuggling cafeteria food to eat at home on weekends), and the "fun" culture became too entrenched to rein in. When customers were being lost, the CEO tried to right the ship by reinstituting the original disciplined culture. Employees recruited during the "progressive" phase felt like they were being punished. Many left and could not be replaced fast enough, and just as spectacularly as it succeeded, the company failed.

Perhaps many factors contributed to the company's failure, but it was obvious to knowledgeable outside observers that the company's leadership failed to recognize the necessary boundaries that should never change. Many of the lies in this book were advanced there. In fact, I visited this company one year before its collapse and was stunned at the near-playground atmosphere when I saw young professionals in work areas bouncing on big rubber balls, enormous tricycles in the reception area, and people using scooters to get around. (I also enjoyed the delicious free lunch available to all the employees).

Does this mean that a company sincerely believing in and attempting to follow the lies will fail? No. What it means is that many senior leaders believing these lies are dangerous to the long-term success of their organizations. Luckily for many companies, their senior leaders recognize the lies.

Be advised that negative consequences can result for openly supporting the positions in this book. If any of the lies addressed in this book are advanced at your workplace, it is best to remain silent about them unless you own the company or are the CEO. Many of the lies are in the "everybody knows, but no one dares to say it" category. The following are the fifteen most commonly repeated lies and half-truths in business today. In no particular order, they are:

◆ ◆ ◆

#1   "Our employees are our most important asset."

#2   "We are a purpose-driven, customer-focused company that exceeds the highest customer expectations."

#3   "Our leaders seek out and hire people who are better and smarter than they are."

#4   "We are an open-door company that encourages open communication up and down. We want everyone to feel free to express their opinions, and we value transparency and honest feedback."

#5   "Diversity, equity, and inclusion (DEI) is essential to our success."

#6   "Our employees are our family, so we place great value on work-life balance. We also want our employees to have fun while at work."

#7 "We offer many educational and professional development opportunities and want team members to use them."

#8 "Our employees embrace volunteerism and enjoy giving back to the community, and they place high value on social consciousness and good causes."

#9 "We believe in modern and up-to-date ways to lead and measure performance. Our leaders embrace data and metrics and see those as the most important tools for determining leadership success."

#10 "We believe the workforce of the future is mostly remote. Accordingly, we will continue to move our teams toward hybrid models. Also, home-based workers will not be at any disadvantages for promotions and advancement opportunities."

#11 "Our excellent strategic plan is the principal guide for our path forward and is key to our company's future growth and success."

#12 "Our acquisition by (or merger with) (Name of Company) is going to make us a better and stronger organization with many exciting opportunities for our employees. There will be few employee changes, and we look forward to working together as one great new team!"

#13 "As CEO, I appreciate our dedicated, engaged, and involved board of directors and welcome their advice, guidance, and counsel."

#14 "Pursue your dreams and find your true purpose in life and your "why," and never, ever stop pursuing them."

#15 "You are too important to us to allow you to leave. Effective immediately, I am making this right. In fact, I had planned on it before this meeting."

◆ ◆ ◆

IN READING THE list, some would think whoever believes these statements are lies is either jaded, cynical, a curmudgeon, resistant to change, or all of the above. The truth is, many senior-level leaders who read them instantly recognize them as false. They also tend to keep silent about them because they pick their battles carefully. That is, until something happens which forces some kind of action. For example, a member of the team they lead expresses critical and negative sentiments to colleagues about them. Upon learning about it, the leader must weigh a response against the company's "free and open communication, both good and bad" policy. Address it or let things slide? In the past, leaders had a clear path: make an example of a disloyal employee. Now it is no longer as clear how to respond.

Or, in the spirit of "leadership transparency," a company uses the increasingly popular and relatively new performance evaluation system where subordinates evaluate their supervisors, and it is communicated to their supervisor's boss. On the surface, this seems like an excellent tool for "in the trenches" feedback, and a good method for exposing tyrannical leaders who, under traditional models, could crush dissent.

The reality is, this system is resented by many

business leaders who might openly extoll its benefits in the "I have nothing to hide" framework. Similar to allowing students to evaluate their teachers (or foxes guarding the henhouse), they know it opens the door for marginally productive employees to stigmatize highly effective leaders who require results, and for popular leaders who might be incompetent to get by unscathed. It also forces effective leaders to pay attention to maintaining popularity, often at the expense of effectiveness. At the very least, it allows the opportunity for planting negative seeds and suspicions about good leaders which previously did not exist.

I have witnessed the negatives of this performance evaluation system firsthand, most recently when I was included in a meeting where a CEO counseled his Chief Operating Officer, the second-highest-ranking leader at the company. The COO had a superb and spotless record until this company implemented the "bottom up" performance evaluation system. Two of his nine direct reports wrote negative statements about him. After the meeting, the CEO told me he knew of the jealous motives of the two malcontents, who had been passed over for promotion to the COO position. What if he did not?

Finally, this book is not about criticizing good ideas and principles. It is about *exposing bad ideas that are communicated as good ones and making them better.* In the following chapters are fifteen of the most often repeated lies in business today (charitably called "half-truths"). Each is examined and discussed. Then, each chapter closes with a proposed solution for effectively and truthfully implementing the statement's well-intended purpose.

HALF-TRUTH #1:

"Our employees are our most important asset."

The best way to find out if you can trust someone is to trust them.
—Ernest Hemingway

Neil McNulty (to the CEO of a 300-employee company): "Many of the candidates we recruit are going to ask about the culture at your company and how you treat people. What can I tell them?"

CEO: "Tell them that our leaders see their people as the most important asset in the company. Nothing gets done without them, so our leaders are expected to treat employees like the gold they are. If someone is considered for a leadership role here, they need to put their team members ahead of everything else."

Neil McNulty: "Okay, ahead of *everything* else?"

CEO: "Well, maybe not *everything*."

◆ ◆ ◆

IF YOU LISTEN to any CEO being interviewed about their company, it is almost *guaranteed* you will hear them say their employees are the company's most valuable asset. The "employees as most valuable assets" expression is a fundamental corporate tenet everywhere. To say or imply otherwise is unthinkable.

If the interviewers were to talk with the employees of that CEO, however, it is a safe bet they would hear something completely at odds with what the CEO is saying publicly. This applies to even the most caring and compassionate CEO.

To most employees, being seen as an asset means being viewed as a "thing" to be used instead of a productive human to engage and lead. Additionally, even the most naive employee knows that the "most" important asset at any company is *money*. Good people are certainly important—but money is the most important thing in a business. *If you cannot pay the bills you cannot employ people.* In fact, you cannot even start up the company. The second most important asset is the product or service the company sells to make the most important asset: money.

Employees as the most important asset to a senior leader is well-intended, but almost insulting to many employees. In fact, at larger companies, the statement usually draws a laugh from the rank and file. They laugh because they stare into computers, tablets, and phones all day, or are on the production line, and are entirely unknown to the CEO and senior leaders, even if the CEO expresses a true personal concern for them. Even the most caring CEOs never really know much about who works at their company, what an individual "in the trenches" does, their hopes and dreams, their family and personal lives, and what they see as their purpose at that company.

I have interviewed thousands of professionals desiring to change companies or entire careers. The top reason for desiring change is a bad boss. The second is being unknown, "invisible," and that their work means very little to the leaders at the company. This simply would not be the case if the CEO's statement was true, that they are the company's "most" important asset. People know and always pay very close attention to their "most" important assets.

I once interviewed a midlevel manager at a large company who stated, "I decided it was time to leave when I was sick and did not go to work, and the following day when I returned, they did not even know I was absent the day before. They either don't care or don't need me." His company's CEO was often in the news because of the size of the company. The CEO spoke often of how his employees are "the most important asset" at his company. I believe he aspired to that, but knew in his heart it was not true, because he could not possibly make it true. Sadly, this situation is more common than the exception.

In business, there are assets and liabilities. The most valuable asset is what an entity cannot survive without. A human being can last months without food, days without water, but only a few minutes without oxygen. A business can survive without many people. It cannot survive long without money. Money is the oxygen of a business.

But how can the business generate money—the most valuable asset—without the people who generate it?

Business leaders can generate it by themselves if necessary. That is why they are the leader, and why the money itself is the most valuable asset. People are the means to the end of acquiring the most valuable asset, but they are not the asset themselves.

Similar to the military commander's "mission accomplishment or the safety of forces" dilemma. Accomplishing the mission is always prioritized over the personal safety of the troops who accomplish it. This is understood throughout the military. A great commander will strive to accomplish a mission with a minimum number of casualties, but the commander must never allow minimizing casualties to become more important than accomplishing the mission.

In business, a leader may truly love and care for

his employees, but the leader knows they are not more important than the business itself. Money and the profitability of the organization (the mission) must always remain more important than the people who work at the company. That's mostly because no matter how much a leader would hate to do so, he/she must be prepared to terminate the employment of non-productive employees because unless money is generated, the entire organization is at risk. This also applies to nonprofits and charitable organizations. Nothing happens without money.

For these reasons, it is always untrue for a leader to state that the employees are the company's most valuable asset, and the employees aren't going to believe it anyway.

◆ ◆ ◆

REPLACING THE LIE WITH TRUTH:

WHAT CAN A leader communicate that truthfully conveys great appreciation for employees? What can cause employees to believe they are valuable, their work is appreciated at the company, and they are making a difference? The company can begin by changing "employees as most valuable assets" to something truthful like this:

"We are a company that cares deeply about our employees and their families. Without them, we cannot succeed as a company, so we value and treasure them greatly. As such, our leaders are encouraged to always consider the impact of their decisions on our employees and their families."

HALF-TRUTH #2:

"We are a purpose-driven, customer-focused company that exceeds the highest customer expectations."

*A truth that's told with bad intent
beats all the lies you can invent.*
—William Blake

Neil McNulty (to the CEO at a private company of 700 employees): "What can you tell me about this company that will make a great candidate jump at the chance to interview here, rather than pursue a career with a Fortune 500 company?"

CEO: "Tell them we are purpose-driven. Purpose is behind everything we do. Every decision we make, every action we take, we first ask ourselves if it is purpose-driven or driven by something else. If it isn't purpose-driven, we don't do it. It's as simple as that."

◆ ◆ ◆

THE ABOVE NOTED answer sounded excellent. And it wasn't true. This company had one of the most *non*-purpose-driven atmospheres of any with which I had worked in almost thirty years. Frankly, the reason for that was its #1 purpose-driven cheerleader: its CEO. According to team members, unless it suited the *CEO's purposes*, it wasn't done.

Lie #2 is actually three lies in one. It combines two of the oldest business lies with a very popular "new" lie in business today. Cleverly, the two older lies are mentioned second and third, as if in the back of the room, and the popular "new" lie is right up front. Today, in order to attract millennials and coming-of-age, Gen Z talent, according to experts, it is imperative that a company's culture values "purpose" as more important than profits and shows some social consciousness.

Business schools across America will agree that the young today do not desire money and achievement in their careers as much as "making a difference in the world," having "purpose," and working at something with "meaning." The other two falsehoods, that a business is "customer-focused" and "always strives to exceed customer expectations," are almost clichés, but *necessary* clichés. What company would dare not claim those two things? However, "purpose-driven" is something that gets attention. It seems new, refreshing, and socially conscious.

The term "purpose-driven" isn't anything new. It simply seems new because it has only recently been resurrected, and most millennials and members of Gen Z were too young to remember its first appearance. Purpose-driven as a theme first arrived on the national scene in 2002 in evangelical Christian circles when church pastor Rick Warren authored a bestselling book titled *The Purpose Driven Life*. Warren's book posits that human beings have an innate God-given desire to make a difference, have purpose, and live a life of meaning. All the themes that are repeated in purpose-driven companies. Interestingly, you rarely, if ever, hear companies mentioning Rick Warren when they speak about being purpose-driven.

Purpose-driven business would be wonderful if it were as true as it is made out to be. Many charitable organizations and nonprofits are truly purpose-driven, and many for-profit companies support worthy causes and charities, but when it comes to selling their products and services, they sometimes must do things that have little purpose, if it means the difference between a profit or a loss, or even staying in business.

A prime example is the tobacco industry. Today,

to their credit, most tobacco companies acknowledge the harmful effects of smoking. Several are also very involved in charitable organizations, something noble and good. Additionally, many of their employment and recruiting materials will say they are socially conscious with research and development, constantly searching for a "safe" cigarette—a noble purpose—and that to join them in that pursuit can be interpreted as purpose-driven. For the most part, they are being sincere.

At least one major cigarette company has nothing but young, highly educated professionals throughout its website, and most young professionals do not smoke. It is a safe bet that many of these young people are sincerely purpose-driven by working toward safe cigarettes. It is also a safe bet that some of their leaders, the senior executives at the company, many with entire careers in the industry, do not want to see smoking go away. If a "safe" cigarette is created, wonderful, but they are not holding their breath (pun intended), and they are not going to retire early or quit the company if one isn't developed.

If a company claims it is "purpose-driven," it should prove it with actions that put purpose ahead of profits. There are companies willing to do that, but they are the exception.

"Customer-focused" is the second falsehood usually paired with "purpose-driven." It is nothing new—it is simply a sharper phrasing of the slogan "the customer is always right," advertised by companies for decades. And even then, as it is now, it is mostly not true.

Today, when one joins most companies, and especially in a sales capacity (and if the company is sensible), they are taught that the customer is often wrong—and to abide by "always right" is costly and foolish. For examples, if the customers are always right, then they should be able to negotiate prices they think are reasonable and the company should always agree. If the customers are always right, then they should always be allowed to return merchandise after using it extensively and receive a refund. There are several ways customers are often wrong.

There are companies which may agree that the customer is not always right, but they will also claim that it doesn't mean the company is not customer-focused. There is some wiggle room for truth here. However, when customers hear the words "we are customer-focused," many are actually hearing "the customer is always right," and that is where the lie remains. Though seeming to split hairs, customers are going to react more negatively toward that company when they ask for pricing they believe is reasonable and do not receive it, or seek to return merchandise and are refused, or some other money-losing proposition for the company.

"Always exceeds the highest customer expectations" is the final piece and dovetails perfectly with the first two lies in the statement. When the customer reads or hears "purpose-driven" and "customer-focused," and added last, but not the least, "exceeds the highest customer expectations," that company has set a very high bar. Too high. The company that sets such a high bar is violating the first rule of customer satisfaction: *under promise and over deliver.*

◆ ◆ ◆

REPLACING THE LIE WITH TRUTH:

A COMPANY SHOULD never communicate all three expectations as givens, and especially in the same sentence. As mentioned, they are establishing unattainable expectations and setting the company up for failure.

Additionally, such statements often immediately trigger suspicions from many consumers and potential customers, challenging them to test the statements by asking for new terms and conditions. If not accommodated, they point to the statement, complain about broken promises, and write poor reviews online. Very similar to the old adage: "when someone says it isn't about the money, it *is* about the money."

The key is for business leaders to communicate a statement that is believable, reasonable, shows the company is deeply concerned with customer needs and wants, but makes it clear it is not going to allow abuse. An example:

"We believe in our company's mission and purpose, both of which drive our most important decisions. We also desire to delight our customers, and we strive to accomplish this by listening to them and doing our best to accommodate their needs and wants whenever possible. By doing so, we often exceed even the highest customer expectations."

HALF-TRUTH #3:

"Our leaders hire people who are better and smarter than they are."

*Better a cruel truth than
a comfortable delusion.*

—Edward Abbey

> **Neil McNulty (to the division general manager of a Fortune 500 company):** "Candidates I approach about this opportunity are going to ask about your leadership. What can I tell them?"
>
> **Division General Manager:** "Tell them I surround myself with people who are better and smarter than I am. I don't want "yes men" and I want to hire people who challenge me. I want them to stand up and speak out to me if they feel strongly about something. I want them to do the same with their teams, and anyone who thinks they are the smartest person in the room doesn't belong here."
>
> **Neil McNulty:** "That is a good philosophy to lead

> by. Why is the position open?"
> **Division General Manager:** "I had to fire the last guy. He wasn't a team player, was too outspoken, and was dragging us down."

◆ ◆ ◆

AS AN EXECUTIVE recruiter, I have worked with some of the most accomplished people in America who emphatically stated how they wanted to hire people "better and smarter than they are" who would speak up, yet they did not tolerate any sort of free thinking or expression from subordinates. However, when I asked the question noted above regarding their leadership, an answer very similar to the above was always given.

It is extremely rare for an executive recruiter to not hear "I want to hire someone who is better and smarter than I am" when asking the person hiring what they are looking for. Or, when asked about their personal career success and what they attribute it to, they usually respond "I have always surrounded myself with people who are better and smarter than I am. They are the reason for my success."

Then, when it comes down to actually selecting the candidate they hire, most will select someone who is *not* "better and smarter" than they are. They select someone who is competent and can do the job but is no threat to their job security. The exception is when they are the owner of the company and have no possibility of being forcibly replaced, or they are hiring their successor. Also, even when hiring their successor, often they will select someone who will not outperform them. They do this so that their companies will always remember them as the perpetual standard of excellence for the company.

Smart executive recruiters do not present their most accomplished candidate when performing a search if that candidate will outperform the hiring authority. They present the "best fit" which, by our definition is someone who can do the job and do it well, will have good personal chemistry with the hiring manager, fits the company culture, and who will *not outperform or outshine the boss.* We know that no matter how much a hiring authority expresses a desire for someone who is better than they are, it is unlikely that we will make a placement if we present candidates who actually are better.

Self-preservation is human nature. No sensible person will hire someone who could replace them in their jobs unless they are specifically intending to hire their replacement. Even then, as just noted, they tend to hire "B" players rather than "A" stars.

The preceding will be strongly denied by some senior leaders. Perhaps they truly believe they actually want people better than they are so that the team can excel. But, either consciously or subconsciously, most decide not to hire them. I have forty years of placement history to prove this statement. Prior to learning this, I actually recruited and presented people who were more accomplished than the person that would be their boss when that individual expressed a desire to hire someone "better and smarter" than themselves. I taught those candidates to show in the interviews what they could do. They did, and very few got hired. So, I decided to experiment by introducing the second-tier candidates first. Qualified, capable, but not superstars. They received offers.

Periodically, I would find someone who was better than the hiring authority, but one who I knew would connect well on a personal level and have a real chance at getting hired. I informed these candidates that they were more accomplished than the hiring authority, and to capture the position, they would need to withhold some of their most outstanding achievements and accomplishments until after they were in the position. Many who followed this instruction were hired. However, most left the positions after only a few years because they tired of reporting to someone less accomplished than they were.

Companies which communicate that their leaders hire people who are better and smarter than they are probably know this is untrue. It is simply another popular claim in leadership today. Good leaders should be absolutely committed to building high performance teams, surrounding themselves with top talent, and promoting their team members' advancement and growth within the organization. Unfortunately, many in leadership positions today do not want the possibility of someone they hire to cause their bosses to think "Hmmm, perhaps we have things backward here." This is especially prevalent in the middle management ranks.

Middle managers have far too much to lose to risk hiring someone who might replace them. Family, mortgages, tuition for private schools, ballet and music lessons, sports, the list is endless. They may say "find me someone who is better and smarter than I am," but when it comes to offers, in my experience, they hire "B" players rather than "A" stars.

◆ ◆ ◆

REPLACING THE LIE WITH TRUTH:

ALMOST ALL BUSINESS leaders will say they seek to hire the best talent possible, but most don't in the end. It is popular and shows self-confidence for a leader to say, "I want to surround myself with people who are better and smarter than I am." Business leaders hire the "best fit," which usually are not people who are "better and smarter" than they are. The exception is those who either don't have much to lose or don't have a lot to gain. Examples include a CEO hiring a successor, or business owners. Truthful companies do not communicate that their leaders hire people who are better and smarter than themselves. Instead, they say something similar to the following:

> "Our leaders always seek out outstanding talent." And "I always try to hire good people who will fit best on the team." And "Our leaders seek the best talent to fit the company and their teams."

HALF-TRUTH #4:

"We are an open-door company that encourages communication up and down, wants everyone to feel free to express their opinions, and where transparency and honest feedback are highly valued."

Never be afraid to raise your voice for honesty and truth and compassion, and against injustice and greed.
—William Faulkner

Neil McNulty (to the owner of a 100-employee company): "What kind of office atmosphere do you encourage?"

Owner: "That is an easy question. We have an open-door policy. No one closes their doors here, ever. We want everyone to see everyone every day, and we also want to see everyone as approachable. When a door is closed, that is a sign of being either antisocial, secretive, or too protective of one's turf—all unacceptable around here."

Neil McNulty: "Well, I hope you take this as humorous—but we are behind closed doors right now."

Owner: "Hmmm, yes, we are. I guess there are exceptions."

◆ ◆ ◆

THE "OPEN DOOR, open communication" lie is one of most frequent policies at companies in America today. The truth: it is just another tool used to appeal to younger workers. Middle managers and senior executives may remain silent about this lie, but most do not like it.

Young people generally dislike chains of command, which they perceive to be "authoritarian," and most have little interest in working for companies where there actually is a protocol that must be followed. Millennials and members of Gen Z have been reared in a world of instant communication to anyone, anywhere, anytime, and unfiltered. To actually be required to go through a boss to get an idea or opinion to someone, or to get noticed and recognized by the highest levels of their company for good work, in their thinking, should not be necessary.

Most middle-to-senior leaders started their careers when all companies had hierarchies, both formal and informal. They always followed a chain of command. To communicate directly with your boss's boss, except for occasional non-business-related matters, was considered highly improper. (And even non-business conversations, if too frequent, were frowned upon). The common term was "end running the boss," and anyone who attempted this assumed huge risks. Getting noticed by the higher ups required political skill to not appear disloyal. A common tactic is to "CC" the direct supervisor in emails with high-ranking leaders. That works for a period of time until the day arrives when the immediate supervisor states clearly to the subordinate "I know what you are doing; run things through me first." When that conversation comes, it is time for that subordinate to find a new job.

"Open door" to younger employees often is interpreted as "I am free to approach anyone at any time." It sounds liberating, and some companies actually allow that, but they are usually smaller, entrepreneurial organizations where the CEO is highly visible every day. Companies beginning at around thirty employees in size have chains of command, even if informal. That's because no matter how open a company is, when a subordinate appears to undermine his or her boss, resentment and trouble results. That is one reason why all Fortune 500 companies have formal chains of command that, if violated, result in serious consequences for the offender.

The open door policy where no one actually closes their door is a relatively new thing. In fact, some companies go so far as to actually *remove* all doors. Anyone who has worked in such a company knows about the interruptions of having people walk right in with the latest grievance or time-wasting idle chat.

It works, but barely.

If one has a door, it is not a bad thing to leave it open most of the time. However, there are times when a door *must* be closed. This is especially so for senior leaders who need private time to think, to speak confidentially on a phone call, or need a private meeting with an employee, customer, or someone else requiring discretion.

Perhaps an "open door" policy is flawed, but what can possibly be wrong with open communication up and down, having a voice that is heard, and transparency with honest feedback?

Much depends upon the definition of "communication." Respectful communication is fine, but the problems happen when the line between respectful and disrespectful is crossed, and it is crossed frequently in open communication companies. This is due again mostly to the current communication free-for-all environment where one is encouraged to communicate with anyone, anytime. Good leaders want their subordinates to speak up and they encourage feedback, but they want it delivered constructively, respectfully, and with the understanding that once a decision is made by the senior, it is carried out enthusiastically by the subordinates, and discussion ends.

Today, decisions are continually debated digitally by subordinates long after they have been made, resulting in suboptimal results. And if the senior tries to bring order to any communication channel, they are frequently viewed negatively by their higher ups when complaints such as "this manager is against open communication and discussion" are submitted. It is a no-win situation—they receive poor results because of open communication and are viewed negatively if an attempt is made to remedy the situation by adding communication controls.

What about transparency and open feedback? What can be wrong with those? Nothing, when done correctly. The problem is it isn't done correctly at most companies. The phrase "in a spirit of transparency" is often heard immediately preceding something negative, similar to the phrase "with all due respect" usually being followed by disrespect. Today, people in workplaces have difficulty maintaining anything confidential, or even determining what should be kept confidential. Company trade secrets, product information, financials, even the personal lives of key executives are on public display. Transparency is out of control and compromised confidentiality is often under its protective umbrella. Here is where executive leadership must step in and define in clear terms what must be kept private and confidential.

Open feedback in business is encouraged today, but those who give it revel in it and those who receive it often detest it. Of course, no one would ever admit as much. In open feedback companies, it is not unusual to be in a conference room where a senior leader says, "Give me some feedback, what do you think?" and a subordinate says, "Well, with all due respect, I think the idea is, frankly, dumb." Egos do not go away easily, so that subordinate will probably pay later.

The rare exception is when a truly self-assured leader replies with something like, "Thank you for this frank and blunt assessment. Interesting. Can you give some details as to why you see it that way?" And then they listen intently and show no signs of irritation. That is the desired outcome with open communication, but it is rare, because it *defies human nature*. Telling a senior privately that they are wrong about something rarely goes well, and publicly saying so, almost never.

People by nature do not welcome criticism, even constructive criticism, no matter how much the senior says otherwise or advocates how it "makes us better."

◆ ◆ ◆

REPLACING THE LIE WITH TRUTH:

TO SUCCESSFULLY IMPLEMENT open door and open communication, it requires corporate discipline. It begins with clearly defined policies that are communicated to everyone on their first day on the job. The policies should clarify the definitions of "open door," "open communication," and "transparency," precisely and coming from the CEO, not HR. For example:

> "XYZ Company is an open-door organization. What this means is, from my personal office to the mail room, office doors should be physically open as much as possible. This not only facilitates an open and welcoming atmosphere, but also a healthier air flow and physical environment. However, one should not enter someone's workspace without invitation. Also, there are times when a closed door is appropriate, such as conversations that should be private. Examples include personal or performance counseling, or conversations where interruptions should not happen. Nonetheless, we shall strive to keep our doors open as much as possible."

AND,

> "XYZ Company is an open-communication and transparent company. Team members should never fear speaking up.

However, a respectful and polite decorum is required. Company leaders are encouraged to solicit input from their teams and instill a spirit where opinions are valued. Also, team members should not fear retribution for stating honest opinions when those opinions have been solicited. However, no one shall use open communication as justification for disrespectful speech, embarrassing others, or insubordination. Finally, all potentially sensitive communications should be private."

AND,

"XYZ Company strives for transparency, especially to external observers, customers, and stakeholders. However, potentially sensitive issues should be discussed with your supervisor before being communicated externally, and nothing that is confidential shall be released without written permission from me or the appropriate officer of the company."

HALF-TRUTH #5:

"Diversity, equity, and inclusion (DEI) is essential to our success."

*Be mindful. Be grateful. Be positive.
Be true. Be kind.*

—Roy Bennett

> **Neil McNulty (to the site leader of a 1,000 employee location):** "Diversity, equity, and inclusion is very important to candidates today. What is your thinking regarding DEI and this site?"
>
> **Site Leader:** "DEI is essential to our success. My management team is very diverse, comprised of a broad range of ethnicities, cultures, orientations, and backgrounds. In fact, a diverse candidate would be ideal for this role and would be more effective."
>
> **Neil McNulty:** "Okay, we will highlight diversity in our search criteria. Tell me, what about diversity in your opinion would make the person hired "ideal" or "more effective" for this role (a production

management position)?"

Site Leader: "Well, I guess anyone can do the role if they have the experience and temperament, but a diverse candidate would be more effective because most of our hourly workers are diverse. They can probably relate better to one of their own."

Neil McNulty's thoughts: Just what does he mean by 'one of their own?'

◆ ◆ ◆

DIVERSITY, EQUITY, AND INCLUSION (DEI) has become one of the most talked about issues in corporate America today. Everyone seems to have an opinion, and they tend to be either fully supportive of DEI, or fully against it. If they are against it, they also tend to be silent unless they own the company, and even then, they keep quiet. To hint at anything other than support for DEI can mean termination, "cancellation," and possible boycotting of a company's products and services.

To be clear, I am fully supportive of DEI; it is good, adds value, and is smart business. However, I have found that most senior-level business leaders are secretly against it in its *current form*, even though they say they are for it in all of its forms.

I am fully supportive of DEI in its *intended* form, not in the current version common in American businesses today. Also, although a good thing for a company, DEI is never "essential" for a company's success unless it is an organization whose core business is DEI-related.

What is wrong with the current version of DEI? The problem is the great lengths businesses go to in order to prove they are supportive of DEI *when DEI should be a natural and self-evident part of a company's culture and never need to be advertised.* It should be expected, similar to ethics and honesty. Additionally, actual DEI is based upon merit and an equal playing field for everyone without considering any other factor that has no bearing on competency or job performance.

A look at the websites of American companies today is instructive, particularly Fortune 500, where almost all will have a statement expressing how important DEI is to the company. If it is assumed that employees are treated with respect and equality, why do they need such a statement? Also, many companies today are hiring a Chief Diversity Officer (CDO), a senior executive whose primary function is ensuring DEI thrives at the company. If DEI is part of the culture, like ethics and honesty, why do they need this executive? Why not hire a Chief Ethics Officer also?

That is a trick question to make a point. Some companies actually have a Chief Ethics Officer— usually to show the world how important ethics are to the company. This usually backfires, causing questions as to why they need such a person enforcing and ensuring ethics if one should naturally expect ethical business practices from that company.

Doesn't DEI make a company better and stronger? Doesn't a diverse culture bring original ideas, perspectives, and competitive advantages to a business? Isn't it good leadership to ensure that team members are always treated equitably, fairly, and inclusively?

Yes to all, and DEI does all that. That is why it is good, but it isn't "essential," which is a lie. What *is* essential is *talent* and its correct application and engagement. DEI thrives naturally when a company hires and properly engages talent, based upon ability and merit, without regard for anything else.

What harm is there in saying DEI is essential—a positive fib, like honoring a host serving horrible food?

The problems begin when DEI, rather than profitability and organizational success, begins to drive decisions. If a host serving horrible food was thinking of opening a restaurant, a kind guest would tell them the food is horrible to keep them from making a big mistake.

In companies with DEI-related issues and problems, a CDO makes great sense. A need exists. Too often, however, a CDO is hired for a non-existent problem. This adds a policy-maker who can burden lower-level managers with unnecessary new policies.

Also, once a CDO is hired, there can never be a future at the company without a CDO. Imagine the backlash if in tough times, the CDO is one of the first to be laid off.

Other considerations:

When a CEO makes a clearly legal and ethical decision, the CDO can state it "doesn't align with DEI policy." Or, after extensive searching, a company manager wants to hire someone they consider to be the best fit for a position, but the CDO says they cannot do so because that particular position was set aside for a "DEI candidate." Exactly what is a "DEI candidate?"

If a company advances true diversity, equity, and inclusion, it will not make business decisions based upon DEI, because fair treatment and mutual respect for all is an expected benefit for working at that company. DEI is so naturally ingrained in the culture that there is no need for website DEI statements or hiring an executive to oversee or enforce DEI. Rewards are based upon merit, achievement, and accomplishment, *and everyone knows it at the company.*

Sadly, the manner in which DEI is advanced today often creates more discord than unity.

◆ ◆ ◆

REPLACING THE LIE WITH TRUTH:

DIVERSITY, EQUITY, AND inclusion is very good in its true and intended form. However, it is frequently not found that way today. Today, many companies go to such great lengths to show how much they support DEI that it often has the opposite of its intended effect. DEI is also not "essential" to businesses, other than organizations whose core product or service is DEI-related. When companies claim DEI is essential to their success, that is immediately questionable.

An organization with true DEI treats everyone fairly, equitably, inclusively, and respectfully, at all times, and without fanfare. Promotions, positions, rewards, and accolades are given for achievement, accomplishment, and merit. Additionally, organizations with true DEI don't need to promote that fact or highlight it. *It is self-evident.* Such a company doesn't need a DEI statement on its website or a CDO. In order to have self-evident DEI, however, senior leaders must clearly define for employees where the company positions itself, how all should treat one another, and prove it through action. As an example:

> "ABC Company's workforce is diverse with a variety of cultures, beliefs, and values, all which give us strength and make us a better company. We believe all our

employees should be treated at all times fairly, equitably, respectfully, and with dignity. Honesty, integrity, and mutual respect shall be the guideposts for all, and no one shall be excluded from any part of ABC Company. All shall have the opportunity to excel and be rewarded for that excellence."

HALF-TRUTH #6:

"Our employees are our family, so we place great value on work-life balance. We also want our employees to have fun while at work."

The truth doesn't change according to our ability to stomach it.
—Flannery O'Connor

Neil McNulty (to the plant manager of a Fortune 500 company site): "This plant is fast-paced, 24/7, and cannot keep up with demand for the products (soft drinks). That is a great thing in a tough economy, but not so good for work-life balance, I would presume. Can you tell me what you do for work-life balance here, under such high tempo operations?"

Plant Manager: "Yeah, we are very fast-paced. In fact, I have not had a day off myself in seventeen days because it's summer and we are on a production run that is unmatched the rest of the year. However, I do believe in balance to keep

> people from burning out."
>
> **Neil McNulty:** "Seventeen days? Aren't *you* burned out?"
>
> **Plant Manager:** (Laughing) "Yeah, I guess I am, you can probably read me like a book! I am exhausted!"

◆ ◆ ◆

BEFORE THE 1980s, there was no such thing as "work-life balance." There was "work," meaning professional life, and there was "personal," meaning home life, and they were kept apart. In fact, business cultures often had strict policies regarding separation of personal from professional life. To even mention attempting to balance the two was considered unprofessional. Professionals were expected to put everything into their work, and personal life was subordinate to work life. If personal life was more important than professional to a manager, they were expected to be non-competitive at their company, and often were passed over for promotions. In fact, management employees were expected to work around the clock if needed, without complaint. If they did express dissatisfaction, they were encouraged to get an hourly position where they clocked in and clocked out and had a set schedule that never fluctuated without advance warning.

After the lackluster 1970s, the early 1980s began

what was eventually called the "go-go decade" for American business. By 1985, Wall Street was booming and became the ultimate employment goal for college seniors studying finance. Movies such as *Wall Street* were immensely popular with their uber-capitalist themes of making money at all personal and ethical cost and pouring one's soul into their work.

Then, around 1987, things changed. The stock market experienced a serious crash, and many lost much of their life's savings (although proving almost insignificant compared to the 2008-2009 Great Recession crash). People began to reexamine their values and question why their employment life was expected to be more important than their family life. Why were they expected to work nights, weekends, and holidays without complaint? And why is it considered unprofessional to prioritize family things like children's soccer games, school plays, birthdays and holiday family gatherings?

The 1987 popular movie *Baby Boom* starring Diane Keaton also illustrated perfectly the growing questioning of those times and the negative results of not sacrificing one's personal life for their career. In this movie, Keaton's character is a high-powered executive who finds herself pregnant, so she attempts to balance motherhood with executive responsibilities. It doesn't work, and she is fired. (There is a happy ending. She starts her own highly successful business).

The term "work-life balance" first appeared around 1988. Initially, it was simply a catch phrase used in recruiting advertisements for hard-to-fill positions. Within about ten years, it became a major corporate culture issue, and any company that did not place high value on it had a difficult time recruiting, especially younger candidates. Today, in general as a group, members of Gen Z place more value on work-life balance than on the company and position itself.

It is unfortunate that work-life balance, for most companies, is just as untrue today as it always has been. Many senior leaders today began their careers in the 1980s and 1990s. They remember placing work ahead of personal life and they paid those dues. The "balance thing" came out of nowhere; they dismissed it as untrue then, and they dismiss it now. They also know that even today, when asked by a candidate in an interview about work-life balance at the company, most interviewers will say it is great, that they are glad they asked, *and then never call that candidate back for another interview.* That's because companies, although unspoken, still want to hire people who prioritize their work and don't want to face possible friction when the inevitable occasions arrive which require longer hours and extra work.

Business leaders today also know that to attract talent, they need to make work-life balance a part of their "pitch." They cannot compete for top talent unless they advertise such perks as liberal time off, work from home days, and, at some companies, even four-day weeks.

What they do not say is when facing deadlines and business goals, it doesn't matter what the perks are. You don't go home or stop working until you meet the deadline and goals.

A good example of this is a well-known and prestigious professional services company that is in the top five for its industry in revenue. It is highly sought by Gen Z college graduates because of its cache: its "brand." On the "Careers" link on its website, it emphasizes many of the latest "work-life balance" perks appealing to young people. These include thirty days of vacation for all, not just for senior executives, two days per week working from home, and liberal leave policies.

The truth is, rarely does anyone at this firm have an opportunity to take thirty days of leave. In fact, most cannot take two weeks. Also, although employees are allowed to work "hybrid" from home, those who do are often regarded as non-productive. Constant rewriting of proposals with hard deadlines, "all-nighters" the day before due dates, deliverables for current projects, late-night "team huddles" that are not effective when remote, etc., are just a few of the things that make a good work-life balance almost impossible at this company.

The company is technically being truthful, because all the good things are available. However, it is the employee's problem to figure out when they have the time to take advantage of them, which is never if one desires to remain competitive at the company.

This is not unique to professional services firms. It applies to all industries. If the work isn't completed when the clock strikes 5 p.m. or the metrics for business success are still pending, work-life balance is subordinated to work. In fact, any company where the pace of business is fast, and competence is required to keep your job, work-life balance is an illusion. Senior leaders all know this.

The preceding does not mean quality work-life balance is not available. It is. There are many types of employment where one can actually enjoy a great work-life balance. With no negative connotation intended, these are usually very large organizations with bureaucracy, or industries where the pace of business is always slow and highly regulated, such as government, utilities, and banking.

Larger organizations in slow-paced and highly regulated industries tend to be great for an excellent quality of life. Their employees get almost all their nights, holidays and weekends free, and rarely, if ever, do they need to stay at work past 5 p.m. There is absolutely nothing wrong with such organizations or the people who seek them. However, in my opinion based upon years of experience interviewing, those who join these organizations should not expect challenging work.

I have interviewed many candidates over the years who, to their truthful credit, told me they were not very ambitious and did not want to work hard or long hours. They also wanted much free time for family life. Nothing wrong with that. I have also sat on a conference panel where a senior executive from a large and highly regulated organization stated plainly "come work for us—you will get great pay and benefits, work Monday through Friday 9:00 to 4:30, never work a weekend, get lots of holidays, and not work very hard. I love it. In fact, I do not do much at all except attend these conferences." The audience laughed, thinking he was joking. I knew he wasn't joking because I had interviewed several people from this organization who were completely bored and wanted to challenge themselves and change employers.

Not all large and multi-layered organizations have slow paces. Some outstanding very large companies have decentralized decision-making and are extremely well run—and cultures of excellence with little tolerance for marginal performers. These include such companies as Procter & Gamble, PepsiCo, General Electric, and Cintas. Their local management teams have real authority, require top performance, and receive it. They support work-life balance, but they subordinate that to delivering consistent value to the customer. It is worth noting that these companies have extremely high personal satisfaction among their employees, and low employee turnover. Frankly, that is because these companies also require exceptional leadership at all levels.

Can smaller, high-intensity, nimble companies have excellent work-life balance? Yes, they can. However, it is not easily accomplished because even the highest-ranking executives must work very hard. The amount of work output of the entire company will correspond to the amount of work output of the senior leadership, which often can mean long hours and weekend work.

What about working remotely and work-life balance?

It is generally good for an employee's personal life to work from home. The problem is that most people who work from home will not—either consciously or subconsciously—work to their maximum potential remotely. People with a boss nearby usually perform at a higher level of effort, and a virtual boss does not have the same effect as when a supervisor can walk down the hall on a moment's notice. For this reason, consider promises of working from home questionable. Most businesses will find a way to get their employees back in the offices. Remote work will be addressed in more detail in a later chapter.

Why is "we want our employees to have fun at work" a lie? What is so bad about working at a company where it's fun?

Companies certainly benefit from having high morale, and leaders should strive to combine high morale with effectiveness. Also, recall the adage "when you love your work, you will never work a day in your life." Loving your work and high morale does not necessarily include fun. Many who love their work will tell you it is far from fun. Workplace fun is good, but effective business leaders know it should not happen too often, and especially not every day. That sounds negative, but there is an excellent reason for that. Recall another saying: "work is not intended to be fun, and that is why it is called work."

Fun, like all things that are pleasurable, should be in moderation. Anything pleasurable that is experienced every day becomes expected, weakens a person, and weakens a company. If every day is fun, when the not-so-fun, tough times happen, as they inevitably do, the stress is very often too much on employees, as demonstrated with the example of the failed Virginia biotech company in this book's Foreword.

Military aviators will tell you there is nothing more fun than flying airplanes. They will also tell you the mission they are training for—possible war—is not fun. A military aviator could go an entire career without ever going to war, but they train with much stress added (not fun) so that they are prepared for the not-so-fun thing should it happen. Smart business leaders do the same thing.

Salespeople have fun when they win sales contests with prizes such as exotic trips, vacations, and cash. However, they also know one reason they enjoy winning so much is all the trials and pain they endured to win, with lost sales, rejection, frustration, and the resilience required to press on through adversity and win.

Medical personnel, first responders, and educators will tell you they love their work. The majority would never want to do anything else. They will also tell you their work is only occasionally fun. Most will say much of the work is painful. This was demonstrated everywhere during COVID-19, especially for medical personnel. Many were exhausted, broken-hearted on a daily basis, and desperately desiring to leave their professions. To their heroic credit, most endured throughout the pandemic. It was hardly ever fun.

Even professions where creating fun is the goal aren't fun. Many would think that being a famous television or movie star would be fun. It isn't. It is hard work. Being on set before the sun rises every day and not going "home" to your trailer until well after dark is not much fun. Then, studying and memorizing the next day's script so you arrive prepared and do not hold up the entire production, and often seven days per week. I was once a guest in an episode of a long-running television show. When invited, I was excited and expected some fun. To my surprise, I had to arrive at 4 a.m. to start "shooting" at 7 a.m. Filming a 30-minute TV episode required over twelve hours of work, broken into very short 20-30 second pieces that were joined together to make a show. Every 20-30 seconds, the Director would shout "cut!" just when all were ready to move to the next part in the script.

One would think being in a famous band would be fun. It is if they enjoy the incredible pressure of knowing that 20,000 people are counting on you to deliver for three hours every night. You cannot get sick, develop a cough, or even have a voice that cracks. Plus, you start traveling to the next city the moment a show ends. Is it any wonder that drugs and alcohol have been a struggle for many musicians? The most successful ones are very disciplined. They watch what they eat and drink, get rest, they exercise, and they avoid alcohol and drugs.

Employers who emphasize how important fun is at their workplaces are either exaggerating at best or lying at worst. Either way, when the expectations for fun are set high, they become very difficult to lower.

◆ ◆ ◆

REPLACING THE LIE WITH TRUTH:

NO ONE ARGUES against enjoying one's work or maintaining high morale at a company. Also, there is nothing wrong with having fun at work every now and then. But when a company advertises that its employees are encouraged to have fun, or that the culture is relaxed and fun, that is a red flag. If true, the company would be on shaky ground during tough times, which come to all companies eventually. If untrue, then the company has lied, and probably lies about other things as well. If a company desires to communicate that it is a great place to work, something along the lines of following is effective and truthful:

> "We encourage our employees to enjoy a life outside of work, to engage in family activities, and to take vacations and holidays without concerns about falling behind in their work. We commit to doing all we can to accommodate such expectations. We also want our employees to be happy and satisfied with their work, to connect socially with each other, and have fun together occasionally. To assist

with that, we sponsor company events and activities on company time where we have good times together."

HALF-TRUTH #7:

"We offer many professional and personal development opportunities and want our team members to use them."

Rather than love, than money, than fame, give me truth.
—Henry David Thoreau

> **Neil McNulty (to the CEO of a 300-person company):** "Being a smaller company compared to Fortune 500 where the environment is resource-rich, what kinds of opportunities can this company offer to a star employee in the way of professional and personal development?"
>
> **CEO:** "Yes, we are smaller, but we have a lot of great things to offer. Tuition reimbursement, a management development program so someone can get promoted, certification programs, all sorts of things. We're small, but big when it comes to taking care of our people. And we encourage them to take advantage of these things, and most do."

> **Neil McNulty:** "Can you give me an example I can share with potential candidates?"
>
> **CEO:** "Let me think on that a bit and get back to you."

◆ ◆ ◆

ALMOST EVERY FORTUNE 500 company actively promotes employee professional development and the programs they offer. Some include this in their advertising. Recently, a large nationwide distribution company ran a series of advertisements which stated, "you can start out packing boxes, and we have a program where you can end up going all the way to the top." In the ads, they have testimonials to prove it. This is a very impressive appeal, but I would be interested in knowing how many apply, how many are accepted, and of those accepted, how many actually get the time to participate. With distribution centers across the USA, the company is certain to have many workers who want in on this opportunity. My guess is that some are happy, and many are disappointed, simply because of how great the program is.

Large companies possess the financial resources to provide many opportunities to their employees. Smaller companies, for the most part, do not. Even so, the larger companies have a problem when it comes to administering such programs. Many people want to participate, so there are problems with that alone.

Great professional development programs are very popular, and if many want to participate, inevitably, decisions must be made as to who participates and who doesn't. The most productive workers usually have ambition and a desire for self-improvement, so they apply for the programs. They deserve to be accepted. However, their supervisors cannot afford to allow their absence. The supervisors buy time—they "slow-walk" the applications, or they persuade the star employee to delay, hoping they (supervisor) are promoted or transferred and are no longer directly involved. The end result is deserving people not receiving what is deserved.

This is not just with business. A good example of this occurred in the 1980s in the military. By 1980, over 90 percent of all US military officers had bachelor's degrees and very few enlisted personnel could even apply for officer programs without at least one year of college.

A well-intended program was created which allowed outstanding enlisted personnel to be accepted into officer candidate school (OCS) if they could pass the screening and had outstanding performance, even without any college. Many highly deserving enlisted personnel applied and were accepted. A problem for this excellent program arose when many commanding officers could not afford to have their best enlisted personnel depart for OCS. They pleaded with their star performers to remain with the current unit until the end of their tour of duty and, being the outstanding people they were, they often did. However, many also decided to leave the service as their obligated service ended, usually coinciding with the end of the current tour.

The preceding is how it often is in large organizations with great development programs. The most deserving employees want the programs and apply for them, but they are too valuable to the supervisor to be absent to participate.

Programs which do not require physical absence, such as online or night courses, are easier to manage, but there remains the problem of taking time off for exams, seminars, and other events requiring physical presence. Additionally, there are often "deal breaker" strings attached such as additional time working at the company for each college credit or the employee must pay back the tuition. Potential candidates are often wary of these and so they don't participate.

The unfortunate result with larger organizations that offer great professional development programs is that most employees who want them will not be capable of participating. The senior leaders know that most can never take advantage of such programs, i.e., they are lies.

What about smaller organizations?

Smaller companies that are privately owned and well-funded can offer great programs and the time to engage them. Their problem, however, is not access-related. The problem they face is lack of rewards for those who complete the programs. For example, if a company has a CEO, a vice president, five supervisors, and sixty employees, what can it do to reward the hourly employees who use the company tuition program to get their degree? Or the employees who gain certifications?

The companies can offer such rewards as cash, trips, and additional leave time, but little in the way of advancement. If the company isn't expanding, then it is training people to go on to other companies to move up. Simply put, small businesses can offer superb professional and personal development programs, but they do so knowing that they will have a difficult challenge retaining the employees who participate. For this reason, relatively few small businesses offer great programs.

Both large and small companies can offer outstanding professional and personal development programs and encourage their employees to take advantage of those. However, many do so knowing not many employees can participate. As such, it is a lie.

◆ ◆ ◆

REPLACING THE LIE WITH TRUTH:

IT IS A very good thing for a company to offer professional and personal development programs. However, companies should not offer such programs unless they are actually accessible to those who want to take advantage of them. Deliberately advertising such programs while knowing very few will have access is misleading and wrong.

If programs are offered which come with commitments, it should be so stated in advertising materials and marketing. Example:

> "Our company strongly supports the professional and personal development of our employees. Accordingly, we offer the following: college tuition reimbursement, seminars and professional conferences, certifications such as Project Management Professional (PMP), management development for hourly employees, personal financial management counseling and resources, free mental health counseling, and

reimbursed gym and athletic fees. Participation in these opportunities is encouraged, but is competitive, may include employee obligations, and could involve work scheduling issues."

HALF-TRUTH #8:

"Our employees embrace volunteerism and giving back to the community, and they place high value on social consciousness and good causes."

*Facts do not cease to exist simply
because they are ignored.*

—Aldous Huxley

Neil McNulty (to the general manager of a large distribution company): "I have been deeply involved in nonprofits, having led three. Your company provided support to all three. Why is it that your company is so involved in social and charitable causes?"

General Manager: "I am glad you asked that. We have a spirit of giving here. Everyone here is cut from the same cloth when it comes to giving back. In fact, this site leads the company out of dozens of distribution centers for volunteer hours. The person we hire for this position *must be willing to volunteer* for community service-type activities."

Neil McNulty's thoughts: Doesn't sound to me like *volunteering*.

MOST COMPANIES WANT to be viewed by the public as generous, charitable, and socially conscious. Additionally, younger employees have been raised with an almost natural inclination for volunteering for what they consider worthy causes. In fact, today in many high schools across America, volunteer hours and community service are required as part of graduation requirements.

Beginning around the mid-1970s, a few American businesses began to realize that participating in charitable, philanthropic, and social causes was not only good for society, but also played an excellent role in marketing products and services. Perhaps the most high profile of these companies was what became one of the most iconic ice cream companies in history. That company started out as a small two-man operation, a "mom and pop" (or "bro and bro") on a farm in Vermont. Its niche was using nothing but natural ingredients to make what many considered the most delicious ice cream anywhere. Additionally, the two founders set out to combine selling great ice cream with making what they believed to be positive changes in the world.

Their small ice cream enterprise grew, not only because they sold delicious ice cream, but also because they involved the company in charitable and social causes. Initially, the company sacrificed much to do so, and executives at other ice cream companies were amused by what they considered to be two somewhat naive guys who looked like hippies putting philanthropy and social consciousness ahead of profits.

The company eventually had a following of millions of loyal consumers who would never think of purchasing any other ice cream. Competing ice cream company executives were not amused anymore, especially when it became a billion-dollar business.

That company was the exception because it was founded upon and has remained loyal to its socially-conscious roots, even while sometimes advancing positions that are controversial. Soon, many companies were on the philanthropic bandwagon. For many, it was not so much to make a positive difference as to make profits, and to attract a younger generation of consumers. Frankly, charity is good business. Today, most Fortune 500 companies have charitable giving and grant making departments, plus many require offices and branches across the company to participate in local philanthropic organizations.

So how is it a business lie to communicate that employees enjoy volunteerism and "giving back" if the companies are highly involved in such causes?

It is a lie because employees who have the volunteer

spirit *do not want to be required or even subtly pressured* to get involved in volunteerism, and those who don't want to get involved at all strongly dislike being told or pressured to do so.

The very existence of volunteer "requirements" defeats the spirit of volunteering. They are being "volun-told." And companies which do not require employees to get involved in charitable and volunteer work will frequently have an underlying and unspoken pressure to get involved. I.e., if the boss is involved in charitable activities, it is not a bad idea to get involved yourself, and it can be a big negative for you if you aren't involved.

Volunteerism is a requirement in many industries, and it is particularly evident in professional services where they serve clients. Accounting firms, law firms, and consultancies usually have volunteer activities as either an official or unofficial criterion to move up in the firm. Visit the websites of the most prestigious law firms in any location and open the links to the senior leadership or partners. Not only will each bio have a list of each executive's professional achievements and accomplishments, but also all the local nonprofit boards and causes the executive is involved in. Such volunteerism is often burdensome when "billable hours" mean something, and only in a confidential conversation would an executive mention how they can barely accommodate the volunteer work which takes away what little free time they have for leisure and family activities.

Additionally, volunteer work usually must pass a vetting process at many companies. Imagine when someone is told they are expected to volunteer for something and so they select a cause or nonprofit aligned with their beliefs. Then, they are told the cause does not present the image the company desires to project.

Employees who do not want to volunteer for anything and hard workers or managers who treasure their free time face less obvious challenges. Many are not considered team players. Ask them what they think when a team of company volunteers is being assembled to work the coming weekend at the local food bank. True, no one is required to participate, and all would understand, especially if they knew about the family reunion or the piano recital. Not a problem at all to not participate.

It isn't a problem until the CEO of the company notes who is present and who isn't when he asks all his volunteers to come up and join him on the food bank loading dock for a photo for the company newsletter. And, doubly unfortunate, the "no show" might be up for a big promotion, and his number one rival is standing next to the CEO in the photo with his arm around him while smiling large. No problem at all.

Even those who are highly productive at their jobs

are often bypassed for promotions and recognition if the company values volunteer participation and they prefer not to get involved in such activities.

Watching television and observing how companies are including employee volunteerism in their advertising is also informative. For example, there is a very large multi-state bank that includes in all its television advertising how their employees are "passionate" about volunteering in their communities. What percentage of the employees really enjoy all the volunteering? The implication is that their employees are unanimously supportive about volunteering when it cannot be true.

The truth is that many hard-working professionals put maximum effort into their regular work and do not want to spend their limited free time in volunteer work. Having served as a CEO/president at three nonprofits, I know what many executives think when they end work at 5 or 6 p.m. and then have a nonprofit board meeting or a charity event they must attend. This doesn't even take into consideration committee meetings or board retreats. Frankly, many are on these boards because their employers take volunteer service into career consideration.

It is important to emphasize how there are some employees who perform volunteer work entirely out of a spirit of generosity. Yes, it is a sacrifice to them, but a sacrifice they willingly and enthusiastically endorse. They are commendable and deserve honor. However, just as many senior-level business leaders view volunteer work as better suited for retirees. They are not being unkind or uncharitable, they are being practical. Their time is a precious commodity, and if they have enough of it to volunteer somewhere, family and personal life often will suffer.

Finally, many larger companies have entire departments whose purpose is to support causes with volunteers, grants, and gifts. Certainly this should be in the company's advertising. However, care must be taken to not raise expectations for those desiring to engage them. Too often for every grant or gift made there are several requests which are denied. Also, the application processes are frequently complex, and the documentation and reports required when a grant or gift is received are often time-consuming and excessively detailed. Simplicity should be the watchword.

◆ ◆ ◆

REPLACING THE LIE WITH TRUTH:

VOLUNTEERISM AND CHARITY are very good for businesses, individuals, and their communities. Every community in America benefits from generous and giving people who spend their time, talent, and treasure helping others. Also, many of the greatest charitable organizations in the world could never succeed without the generous contributions made by their corporate sponsors and volunteers who are often busy executives, managers, supervisors, and hourly workers. The truth, however, is that many who work hard at full-time jobs do not enjoy volunteer work because of limited free time, and they dislike being directed or pressured into it by their employers. Some enjoy the volunteering, many don't. The volunteerism lie can be replaced with truth by a statement like this:

"At (Name of Company), many of our team members participate in charitable and philanthropic causes and organizations. Our employees work hard at their jobs, and they sacrifice much family and free time in their volunteer activities. They do this entirely on their own without any pressure from the company. To recognize and thank them, we hope you will join us at our annual volunteer appreciation luncheon/dinner. Details are listed below. Also, if you or your organization seeks financial or volunteer support in a charitable cause or activity, please visit our "Giving Back" link on our website."

HALF-TRUTH #9:

> "We believe in modern and up-to-date ways to lead and measure performance. Our leaders embrace data and metrics and see them as the most important tools for leadership success."

There are three types of lies: lies, damn lies, and statistics.
—Benjamin Disraeli

Neil McNulty (to the CEO of a 200-employee company): "What do you use to measure the success of your subordinate leaders?"

CEO: "Key Performance Indicators (KPIs) are used to measure success. The numbers are everything. We don't need charismatic leaders and great talkers who do not deliver the numbers. Frankly, I don't care if someone is a lousy people person if they deliver the numbers."

Neil McNulty: "We can probably find someone for you who is both an inspiring leader *and* delivers the numbers, but they might not be here long-term if the leadership culture isn't that important."

CEO: "That is great if you can, but it isn't necessary.

> The numbers are a "must have," and the people skills are an added benefit. Our leaders are oriented toward numbers—and that is what I want them to focus on."

◆ ◆ ◆

ANY BUSINESS LEADER understands the basic difference between leadership and management. The fundamental difference, they will say, is that leadership involves how you deal with people, and management involves how you use things. Unfortunately, that is about all most business leaders understand about leadership unless they come from an environment that places greater importance on leadership than management. The CEO quoted placed more importance on management than leadership. To his credit, he did not hide that fact. However, the position he tried to fill became a "mission impossible" as we say in the search business. The candidates who met him did not want to work in a place where numbers are more important than people. They acknowledged the importance of delivering the results, but not at the expense of how to treat people.

Based upon years of working with all kinds of companies, I believe leadership remains more important than management when it comes to the long game. Many will disagree with that. In fact, I have had more than one CEO who came up through finance (numbers-focused, not people-focused) tell me that the biggest mistake a modern CEO makes is to be more focused on leadership (people) than management. They usually say technology has reduced the importance of the human dimension. That is believable, but untrue.

Today, many CEOs came up through finance and accounting and are great with data, but many of those are also poor leaders. Prior to 2000, most CEOs came up primarily through sales and marketing, the people side. Accounting, finance, engineering, and human resources have always been important, but they rarely led to the top position unless the CEO did a "tour of duty" in those departments, (which they often hated).

Now, hard numbers, metrics, KPIs, and data are becoming the CEOs. Yes, they are "successful" with good numbers, but what is frequently not a concern is the hidden cost in employee turnover if they are poor leaders.

Turnover is one of the costliest expenses to a company and isn't easily recognized as such. In numbers-focused companies, they often burn through one person after another as easily as using up raw materials. The expense is willingly absorbed with hardly a shrug. In fact, there is a Fortune 50 consumer products company that has an incredibly high turnover of managers and yet the senior leaders don't change anything, almost wearing high turnover as a badge of honor. The people who join that company know they are looking at two to three years in a crucible of numbers-driven management, but they also know it is a superb resume enhancer to have spent time at that company because of the known adversity and resilience required to succeed.

I have interviewed literally hundreds of finance, accounting, and numbers-focused professionals. I usually ended up dreading sending them on interviews because, for the most part, they were either too quiet, too introverted, or unable to carry on a conversation with a stranger. Many were also not good leaders, and there is absolutely nothing wrong with that. The problems occurred when they were being interviewed for leadership roles. There were some who were both numbers-focused and great leaders, but only a small percentage.

Marketing and sales success, on the other hand, requires understanding people: how they feel, how they relate, how they buy, and applying that knowledge to get people to act in a desired way. In other words, by mostly leading them.

So, where is the lie in all this?

The lie is when a company claims their leadership fully embraces metrics, data, KPIs, as the best measures of success. Perhaps the newer CEOs are metrics-focused, *but their direct reports usually aren't.* Many senior leaders dislike data as the primary measure of success because it rarely takes into account things such as how many people quit the company while achieving last quarter's superb numbers.

Perhaps the biggest strategic weakness of organizations today is lack of leadership, beginning with the CEO. The good news is that many companies recognize this and are doing something about it. The bad news is that the actions taken are usually the blind leading the blind.

For example, I recently worked with a 700-employee company with multiple business lines. The CEO, a "numbers and data" guy, admitted to me that most of the company's management level leaders had never had any kind of leadership training. These managers were measured strictly by their production numbers, and high turnover in their ranks resulted. However, at my urging, the CEO was willing to try some leadership training for them.

Instead of interviewing experienced leadership consulting firms run by people who had actually led similar organizations successfully—such as former CEOs and senior military officers—the CEO engaged a firm led by a thirty-year-old technology entrepreneur whose only achievement was starting up a successful dating website. An impressive accomplishment for a young entrepreneur, but absurdly weak for teaching frontline production and operations leadership to managers and supervisors.

This company's managers traveled to New York to attend a one-week course at fifteen thousand dollars apiece, taught by twenty-somethings who had never led anyone. First-class leadership training from local firms was available, and what they received had little applicability, with much self-analysis and little actual leadership training.

The preceding example is not uncommon. CEOs are bombarded with the latest in leadership when leadership fundamentals, like human nature, do not change. And one does not need to go far for excellent leadership training. In fact, almost every city's Chamber of Commerce offers outstanding leadership development programs.

◆ ◆ ◆

REPLACING THE LIE WITH TRUTH:

METRICS, DATA, AND KPIs are all very important. No business can operate successfully without those. However, a trend is happening across American business today where CEOs are paying closest attention to numbers and data while lowering the importance of leadership and the human component. Management of things is becoming more important to CEOs than leadership of people. To compound this is a growing lie that leaders at all levels embrace this thinking. Numbers-driven CEOs might embrace data as the best measure of success, but their subordinate leaders usually do not.

What should a leader say that reflects accurately the importance of metrics but also takes into account the leadership side of the business? A numbers-minded leader can say something like this:

"We believe that metrics, KPIs, and data are the best measures of success, and we rely heavily on those for our management decisions. However, in all our decision-making, we consider the impacts our decisions will have on our people, our employees, and their families. Our employees deliver the numbers which define our success. As such, we will never put data and metrics as more important than our employees' welfare unless the company's very existence is at risk."

HALF-TRUTH #10:

"We believe the workforce of the future is mostly remote. Accordingly, we will continue to move our people toward hybrid models. Also, home-based workers will not be at any disadvantages for promotions and advancement opportunities."

*In a time of deceit, telling the truth is
a revolutionary act.*
—GEORGE ORWELL

> **Neil McNulty (to the vice president and general manager of an office location for a Fortune 500 company:** "With COVID behind us, many companies are requiring their office workers to return to their pre-COVID work locations. What are your thoughts about that?"
>
> **Vice President:** "COVID proved we can succeed with good people working from anywhere. I will hire anyone who is good, and at any location, as long as they get the work done. In fact, it's the future."
>
> **Neil McNulty:** "Okay, great. So, you want to interview some strong remote candidates?"
>
> **Vice President:** "Sure, but only as a last resort."

◆ ◆ ◆

LIE #10 is perhaps the most pervasive lie today. Yes, COVID proved that disciplined, hard-working people can work successfully from anywhere. Also, COVID proved that companies are capable of surviving by closing physical offices and having people working remotely.

Additionally, watch any business channel and listen to the "experts." They will all say the same thing:

"Workers want to work from home, and companies who do not allow that will not be competitive for top talent. The future of work is remote." Usually, these self-styled experts are basing their opinions on what they are reading and seeing, and not from private conversations with business leaders.

The unspoken and unpopular truth is that many CEOs, business owners, and senior leaders want people back in their offices, *and they will not change that position.* They are simply waiting for the right time to drop the hammer. And as of the year of this book's publication, the "warning lights" are showing. To these leaders, working from home is a lingering reminder of the COVID dystopia, and they desire a full return to pre-COVID normalcy. That is not far off even without an economic downturn, and when the next recession comes, and it will, those workers who avoided companies requiring a return to offices will regret it.

Nonetheless, many of these same leaders are saying they embrace remote or hybrid work. This is part of the fictional work-life balance narrative addressed earlier and needed to recruit younger professionals. Over time, policies and requirements are put in place where work cannot be accomplished from home, but without ever formally eliminating the remote option. Examples include projects requiring close coordination to a level that is ineffective when remote, or use of equipment and technology that is located in the office and not permitted offsite.

Many businesses which were in offices pre-COVID can do fine with a continuing remote workforce, and companies founded during COVID can be remote indefinitely. The issue is that many companies which were in-person pre-COVID will not return to *full productivity* again until a return to in-office. A supervisor physically nearby cannot be duplicated remotely, and people tend to work harder when the person who can fire them sees them multiple times per day, and not just on a screen.

The preceding is exactly why most workers want continuing remote work. COVID was the perfect excuse to get away from the boss. And many of those who say they can perform better remotely because of fewer distractions or no commuting time are using convenient and believable half-truths. The principal reason they want remote work is lack of direct supervision. This is also why many business leaders who say they support and embrace a remote workforce are untruthful.

Unless a person is a writer, programmer, sales representative, or some other type of profession which is intended to be performed solo, it is usually false when one claims they can be more productive in a remote role.

In the executive search industry, long before COVID, many consultants left their offices to start their own consultancies working from home. Or they asked their supervisors if they could work from home because search work is mostly all computer and telephone.

The vast majority failed. To succeed as a search consultant requires much personal discipline, and each day is carefully planned. Even the most disciplined in-office search consultants have difficulty succeeding from home. The same principles apply to many industries. In-person workers are generally far more productive than remote.

Additionally, people who work best from home generally tend to be loners by nature. They enjoy being away from people.

There is nothing wrong with desiring to work solo, but people should not be surprised when they do not receive leadership roles or advancement. That brings us to the second half of this lie: that remote employees are not at a disadvantage for promotions, advancement, and competitive assignments. They are.

CEOs and senior business leaders know that to lead effectively, you must be someone who seeks out leadership roles and enjoys working with and around people. They also know that employees who regularly see the company's influencers in-person have the highest probabilities of creating good relationships with those influencers.

It can work both ways. An in-person worker could create a poor relationship with company influencers, but when selecting people who will run important things, most leaders tend to select people they know. If two people are fully capable, and one is in-person and one is remote, the in-person employee has the advantage unless that person has a poor relationship with the influencers.

Working remotely does not facilitate deep personal or professional relationships, and that is the primary reason why remote and hybrid are not the future of work. Remote may never disappear entirely, but the trend is moving toward companies with a small core group of key leaders who are operating from company offices directing remote workers who are entirely happy being left alone *and not advancing in their careers.*

Nonetheless, the majority of companies will eventually require almost everyone to return to offices, and that is where the lie exists.

REPLACING THE LIE WITH TRUTH:

WORKING REMOTELY MAY never disappear, but it will become much less common. During COVID, companies which were started up around a remote model will most likely not change, but they are a small sector.

Companies which sent workers home due to COVID will continue to allow remote or hybrid work for a few, but most will be required to return to offices, and certainly so if they desire to be competitive. Remote work reminds business leaders of the pandemic, and most leaders want a return to pre-COVID normalcy. Personal relationships will return to the workplace, and it is happening already across the American business landscape.

The following is a truthful statement that might also attract younger workers who want remote work:

"Prior to COVID-19, our company was entirely in-person and within our company locations. The pandemic required us to send everyone home, and to keep from losing their jobs, everyone worked from home. All performed magnificently under very difficult circumstances! Now, the time has come for us to return to our offices and reconnect in-person with our colleagues and team members. However, at the present time, we will continue to consider remote and hybrid work on a case-by-case basis."

HALF-TRUTH #11:

"Our excellent strategic plan is the principal guide for our path forward and is key to our company's future growth and success."

A man, a plan, a canal, Panama
—Unknown

Neil McNulty (to the board chair of a large nonprofit corporation, February 2020): "I read the strategic plan (SP) online. The organization is now approaching two years in on the five-year plan. How are things playing out?"

Board Chair: "Excellent, right-on target! A few minor setbacks, but, overall, everything is going according to plan. By 2023, I fully expect that we will have fulfilled the plan very closely."

♦ ♦ ♦

EVERYONE KNOWS WHAT happened one month later, in March 2020. COVID-19 put this organization's strategic plan on the electronic file shelf to collect digital dust, along with all other SPs (unless the planners had planned for a global pandemic). This was also true for all SPs on September 12, 2001 and, to a degree, October 8, 2023.

The truth is that it doesn't require catastrophe or major world upheaval to derail strategic plans. All that is required is time. Business leaders with deep experience know that most SPs are not worth the time, effort, and resources they consume, but to admit that would be another example of business blasphemy. Business schools, consultants, and corporate boards all preach that strategic planning is essential for strategic level leadership. The truth: good strategic plans are useful, but a company can thrive without one. It isn't essential, and most successful executives know it. And well-composed good SPs are rare. In fact, SPs often *hurt* organizations by stifling initiative for seizing unplanned opportunities. "Doesn't keep us on our SP, so don't go down that rabbit hole" is heard often. Interestingly, the strategic level leaders believed to benefit most from SPs often succeed because they *ignore* their company's SP. They know that most plans are going to change radically, in the same way that military leaders know that most military plans change as soon as the first shots are fired.

As an executive recruiter, I have been engaged often to find C-suite executives and, invariably, the client organization emphasizes "extensive strategic planning experience" in the position requirements. Ironically, when interviewing prospects, I know that when a candidate states they believe strongly in strategic planning, they are saying what they know is needed to get hired, i.e., lying. In fact, having been a CEO on three occasions myself in addition to being a business owner, sometimes I would say to a CEO prospect "Okay, I will not use your answer against you, but how many of your SP outcomes were close to the plan?" They would usually laugh, because we both knew the answer. And these leaders were leading successful companies.

So much for the saying: "failure to plan is planning to fail."

Having seen many strategic plans and then subsequent attempts to follow them, I believe a reliable rule of thumb is that with each year, approximately 20 percent of the plan becomes obsolete. As such, by the fourth year of a five-year SP, 80 percent of the original plan is no longer applicable. Humorously, there are many organizations that plan for SP obsolescence, so they shorten the SP horizon to three years. Then, they are confounded when two years in, 40 percent is irrelevant, and by the third year, only 40 percent of the original plan remains viable, causing stakeholders to wonder why there was a SP in the first place. That written, a three-year plan is usually better than all other time horizons.

Another tool used for combating strategic plan irrelevance is to make the SP a living document, "flexible, and easily adjusted to changing realities." Seems to make sense. Then, what usually results is a constantly changing SP, and constant changing of an SP means there is no plan at all, other than a "plan to make changes to a plan."

To be fair, some strategic plans are useful. Also, there is value in planning what an organization should look like three or four years in the future. However, based upon my experience interviewing successful strategic leaders, SPs should not be detailed. An SP should have three to four broad, achievable, and *visionary* goals, not five to seven (and specific) goals most common in SPs. And successful plans tend to leave out the details of the "how." These plans will have basic information of the "how" but will empower subordinate leaders to figure out the details.

SP development processes are usually drawn-out, multiple-meeting, painful experiences for participants. An external facilitator is usually brought in, a consultant who is an expert at SP creation. Most SP facilitators know deep inside that the end product will probably become irrelevant before its time horizon is reached, but they are under no obligation to reveal that opinion to their client organization.

Connected closely with strategic planning is an organization's mission statement. The creation of a mission statement is usually the first component of the strategic planning process. "Start with the end and work back from there" is heard often. If one were to ask many CEOs what they thought of their organization's mission statement, many would say they don't know what it is!

A review of mission statements often reveals lofty platitudes, superlatives, and clichés that, when taken as a whole, sound great but mean little. Many CEOs, for the most part, secretly believe a mission statement is aspirational and unrealistic. They also quietly wonder why it needs to be reviewed with each new SP. If the organization sells the same products or services as it always has, what is the point in changing the mission statement?

An effective (and believable) mission statement is simple, unchanging, brief, direct, and similar to the military where the objective of an operation is defined concisely and precisely. It leaves out the exaggerations, superlatives, and the "how." Example:

Mission Statement: "To become and remain America's preeminent and preferred provider of (fill in here the principal product or service provided) products and services."

When a CEO or senior leader states they are confident their organization's strategic plan will come to fruition, they are often lying. Also, when referring to their organization's mission statement, many will never admit they don't even understand what it says or means.

◆ ◆ ◆

REPLACING THE LIE WITH TRUTH:

EXPERIENCED CEOs HAVE seen enough strategic plans to know that most become obsolete quickly. These CEOs also believe that the manner in which a lot of strategic plans and mission statements are developed waste time and resources, but to say so is too contrarian. However, there is value in a well-developed strategic plan. The problem arises because very few are well-developed. Accordingly, the most successful senior-level leaders I have observed plan day to day, week to week, and month to month. They know the world can, and probably will, turn upside down, rendering plans with more than a one or two-year horizon as obsolete. If they have an SP, they use the model the military uses: direct, brief, narrow, easily understood, and with three or four achievable, clear, and realistic goals. "Mission-type" plans which establish the leader's intent and empower subordinate leaders with the freedom to determine the "how." These plans lack details by design, replacing the detailed planning that is espoused by traditionalists.

"Our planning strategy is simple and straightforward: each of us, every day, will work hard and do our best to accomplish our overall goal of delivering the greatest value to our customers. We will not be rigidly tied to one unchanging, inflexible plan. Instead, we will be guided by the following general objectives:

1.

2.

3.

4.

We will seek out and seize opportunities that make sense, even if there was not a previous plan for pursuing them. Whatever the outcomes, we will accept if there's excellence, and correct if there's not. Additional planning guidance is outlined here (link to a two-page SP)."

HALF-TRUTH #12:

"Our acquisition by (or merger with) (Name of Company) is going to make us a better and stronger company with many exciting opportunities for our current employees. There will be very few employee changes, and we look forward to working together as one great new team!"

Resolve to be a master of change rather than a victim of change.
—Brian Tracy

Neil McNulty (to the CEO of a private company with 300 employees): "Great hearing from you, (Name), are you calling about another key position you want filled by my company?"

CEO: "Sort of. This must remain highly confidential. I'd like you to place *me*. I just received word that we are being merged with another company. The owner says my job is solid—even says that I will run the larger new company, but I am not taking any chances. I need to get out of here."

◆ ◆ ◆

THE PRECEDING CONVERSATION is one I have had many times over forty years as a search consultant. A CEO or senior executive from a company where we have placed talent contacts me desiring to leave the company, and 75 percent of the time, the reason given is due to a merger or acquisition.

Frankly, it is amazing to me that high-ranking employees of companies being merged or acquired actually believe that their jobs are safe. I have witnessed literally dozens of "M&As," and it is the rare exception when the new entity's leaders do not order significant employee changes, which frequently involve terminations. This is particularly evident at the C-level. The acquiring company, or larger merger partner, is not going to have room for two of every kind of senior leader. Furthermore, companies which acquire other companies, for the most part, do not acquire something unless they are going to change it.

Darkly amusing, the public story of an M&A usually involves a lot of positive statements (i.e., "spins") such as how much the current employees at both companies (acquirer and the acquired) are looking forward to working together and all the exciting and positive changes they expect to happen. Within this context, it is almost guaranteed there will be a joint statement by the partner CEOs about how they will now serve as co-CEOs, or that one of the two CEOs is totally content with their demotion to Chief Operations Officer or Executive Vice President of the new entity. (Most calls to headhunters come from the demoted executives).

Why would the acquiring company or merger partner lie so brazenly? Most often, it is because the most valuable components to the acquiring company involve retaining specific individuals at the acquired company. *There are* people whose jobs are safe. In fact, very safe. These fall into two categories. (1) Lower-level supervisors and workers who actually make the product or provide the services at the company (they get the work done), and (2), senior or special leaders who have so much knowledge, experience, or part of the "brand" that they cannot be sent away dissatisfied or angry. These are powerful people who can cause a lot of harm (lawfully) by being forced out.

The preceding two categories of employees have leverage and should actually stick around. What often happens is the supervisors and workers simply have the letterhead on their paychecks changed, and their employment continues relatively unchanged. The special key employees, after they have offered up their knowledge and experience, are frequently offered significant financial incentives to leave the company on their own. However, such separation agreements usually involve restrictive covenants and a lot of non- competition and confidentiality clauses that can severely limit the executives' ability to get hired somewhere else. Such agreements should always be reviewed by an attorney before signing.

Either way, anyone in a merged or acquired company should be wary and take precautions to ensure paychecks do not stop. Most often, C-level employees at acquired companies lose their jobs, and any area where there is duplication can expect layoffs. Don't believe the lie that all is safe unless you are a lower-level employee actually doing the company's work, or you have key value to the company that is highly unique (which isn't many).

◆ ◆ ◆

REPLACING THE LIE WITH TRUTH:

WHEN A COMPANY is being acquired or merged with another organization, there are personnel changes coming. If someone occupies a senior management role at the acquired organization, there is an increased probability they will be forced out in the foreseeable future. To believe otherwise is wishful thinking, and to believe corporate statements saying all will remain unchanged is incredibly naive for a senior manager. If told all is well, an executive should have a new employment contract written up proving it.

What can a company communicate that is honest yet keeps valuable people from leaving? Frankly, nothing. When employees fear losing something extremely important to them, like their jobs, they take action, just as noted in the first chapter of this book. However, when employees are told they will not lose their jobs and then lose them later, they are much angrier and can cause much more harm than if they had simply been told the truth from the start.

The following is an example of a statement which conveys truth yet might keep key people around:

> "As you know, our company is being acquired by (or merged with) (Name of Company). I realize this has caused some anxiety with some of our team members. In that regard, I have been informed that our new organization will do its best to make the transition with the least disruption. However, nothing is guaranteed. My hope is that each of you sticks around to see how things play out, because it might end up being fantastic. Time will tell. In the meantime, I ask that you please work as hard as you always have. It is greatly appreciated. Please feel free to communicate with me directly, or with your supervisor, to discuss any concerns."

HALF-TRUTH #13:

> "We appreciate the dedicated, engaged, and involved board of directors we have and welcome their advice, guidance, and counsel."

Add a few drops of venom to a half-truth and you have an absolute truth.

—Eric Hoffer

Neil McNulty (to the CEO of a 700- person company): "I see you have some very notable and distinguished people on your board. Impressive. How engaged are they, and do they help you out or get in the way?"

CEO: "I will tell you the truth. My board is a group of well-meaning, very high-profile people. That, I appreciate. What I do not like is how some of them really think they know what they are talking about with our company but actually know very little about what we do here. That means they can come up with some pretty bad ideas and unworkable suggestions from time to time which I have to diplomatically

> disregard, and without appearing to ignore them because they are my bosses. I wish they would only offer advice or get deeply involved upon request."

◆ ◆ ◆

THIS LIE IS exclusively a CEO lie and is the "nuclear option" of all lies. It is blasphemy for CEOs to ever say or imply anything other than positives about their boards. If they don't, they will be fired. It is as simple as that.

It is rare for me to speak confidentially with a CEO who does not secretly wish at least one or two of their board members would not get involved in their company as much as they do. It usually isn't anything personal. Rather, it is mostly a matter of being accountable to people who the CEO thinks lack true understanding of the company. However, every CEO will say publicly how they appreciate their boards. This is particularly evident at annual meetings where CEOs often give their boards praise, awards, and recognition. It is eerily similar to when someone testifies before a congressional committee. They always begin by thanking the committee for the "opportunity" to testify, and it quickly becomes painfully obvious they prefer to be anywhere else.

For the most part, no matter how progressive, many CEOs want to run things their way, be in charge, and not be told what to do. Some have worked their entire careers seeking the title "CEO" and do not want unsolicited advice or assistance. Some also view boards as telling them how to run the company even though board members will say they never tell the CEO how to run things. This applies to even the most distinguished, high-achieving board members who have much to offer and want to offer it. And that is where the problem lies.

Many CEOs think board members should offer advice, not direct, unless the CEO is failing. And they should offer advice primarily upon the CEO's request. Otherwise, they should remain in the background.

High value board members look only at the big picture and do not inject themselves into the daily activities at the companies they serve unless there is a very good reason to do so. They realize they operate with, at best, only about 20 to 30 percent of the information, so they defer to the CEO for operational or tactical-level matters. They offer input when the CEO asks for it unless, as mentioned, he is failing and needs direction.

Problems arise when board members start out strategic and big-picture-minded, as it should be, and over time morph into day-to-day involvement and getting "into the weeds." This occurs most often with members who desire to appear informed, engaged, and relevant, but, in fact, are not very knowledgeable.

Often, they cram all their board meeting advance reading in the two days immediately before meetings and offer unworkable suggestions as a result.

A recent example was a CEO I worked with who was running a large nonprofit charitable organization which resettled refugees and immigrants. This CEO shared with me how a board member called him and asked what the organization was planning for supporting a refugee matter over one thousand miles away. It was not possible for this organization to do so due to funding and logistic issues, which a board member should have known. When the CEO informed him that the organization could not support the distant need, the member responded negatively and implied that the CEO was not doing his job.

The intention might be to not tell the CEO what to do, but many boards do. The exception is the very rare CEO the organization will collapse without—the leader who has skills and knowledge no one else possesses or is the "brand" of the organization. With these CEOs, boards tread lightly. But they are few and far between.

Regarding the board's sincere desire to help: most CEOs genuinely appreciate that. However, these CEOs know what they need to do and how and will ask for help if they need it. Excellent CEOs are skilled at making things successful with minimal assistance, supervision or direction.

◆ ◆ ◆

REPLACING THE LIE WITH TRUTH:

OBVIOUSLY, THIS LIE is dangerous to any CEO who admits it. No CEO would ever express anything except appreciation, respect and support for their board of directors unless there is nothing to lose, such as retiring or moving on to another opportunity.

Board members are viewed by most CEO's as their bosses, even though many board members will deny that characterization. Most members want to be viewed as a positive resource, and they want the CEO and company to succeed. Board members also have a fiduciary responsibility that can land them in legal trouble if the company fails through some kind of negligent or nefarious act. They need to pay attention to what a CEO is doing. Accordingly, some give unsolicited advice or direction. When this occurs, tension can develop.

A CEO would be truthful to communicate something like the following regarding their board:

"I appreciate the board of directors at our company. Each member is distinguished, highly accomplished, and brings great value to the organization. I view our board as a tremendous resource that is always there when I need it. When I ask for guidance, they never fail to assist, and they put special confidence in me by not getting involved in the day-to-day workings of our company, which they faithfully entrust to my stewardship. They set realistic and far-reaching goals for our company and trust me to fulfill those. I am honored to serve with them."

HALF-TRUTH #14:

"Pursue your dreams, find your true purpose in life, your "why," and never stop pursuing it."

I've looked at life from both sides now, from up and down, from win and lose, and still somehow, it's life's illusions I recall, I really don't know life at all.
—Joni Mitchell

> **Neil McNulty (to a senior executive at a Fortune 500 company):** "I read that you delivered a college commencement speech recently. What did you tell the graduates?"
>
> **Senior Executive:** "I told them they have the entire world at their feet, that they should not allow anyone to define them, and they should find their purpose in life and give it everything they have to make it happen. And, to never give up on pursuing their hopes and dreams, to press on through the adversity that is bound to happen."
>
> **Neil McNulty's thoughts:** "That advice is what has driven tens of thousands of young people into poverty before the age of thirty."

◆ ◆ ◆

THIS LIE IS very dangerous because there is also some truth in it. The danger resides in the fact that the people who are most vulnerable to the lie, the young, between ages of twenty-two and thirty, have not experienced enough life to discern between truth and reality.

If you research career and employment-related thought leaders and influencers and watch their videos, it is certain you will hear almost all of them advancing the unrelenting pursuit of dreams, finding purpose, and the importance of living these if you desire a satisfying life. In the last ten years, there has also been a new catchphrase in the self-discovery world: "finding your "why." The premise is that until you find your true purpose in life, your "why," and have a career that is related to it, you will never be totally content professionally—and maybe even personally as well. There is a grain of truth to that. What is rarely, if ever, said is that reality usually supersedes dreams for most.

Coming from a faith background (Roman Catholic, to be specific), I personally believe everyone has a purpose, a calling, and that God has given each human being gifts for fulfilling those. That written, this book is not about faith or religion—it is a secular book about preventing career-related disasters. And, having interviewed thousands of career changers over forty years, I have seen more than enough disasters. More than two-thirds are directly related to pursuing one's dreams at the expense of family, friends, and personal finances. And, most often, the pursuit of dreams was at the advice of a guru, mentor, or influencer who said they should never give up on their pursuit.

Dreams can and do come true and making them reality usually requires immense sacrifice and overcoming tremendous adversity. Every famous and successful person suffered much to get where they are, unless it was handed to them through a trust fund, family business, or they were a one-in-a-million person where things simply fell into line.

For the remainder of the 999,999, they either gave up on their dream, pivoted to a different approach, or followed the dream into bankruptcy. Most of these were told often by loved ones that they needed to make a change, but they made the change only when they were forced into it.

Since 1984, I have counseled and placed into civilian careers military people leaving active duty. They have served their country and deserve satisfying civilian employment. There are many programs and resources available to them but, sadly, over 50 percent are still either unemployed or underemployed three months after their last active-duty paycheck. I know the reason for that. The reason is because all military-to-civilian career transition programs teach that the first step to a satisfying civilian career is to identify what you want to do—and pursue it. What they should be teaching is to pursue what you are *qualified to do*, and from there, *while earning a paycheck*, figure out what you really want to do and then make a plan to find it.

Few people will give advice that people do not want to hear. For military in career transitions, many of whom have sacrificed much in service to the nation, finally doing what you want to do is appealing and exciting. Unfortunately, that pursuit almost always results in unemployment and underemployment, because they learn quickly that they are searching for a needle in the haystack.

The advice that should be given at college commencements or in military transition classes is that a dream should be pursued to the point in time where the cost of pursuit is negatively affecting one's life. To many, that means they are already past that tipping point.

The bottom line is this: someone should pursue a dream, their "why," their "purpose," their "calling" career only when it does not negatively affect their lives or those who are important to them.

To say to someone under the age of thirty to never give up on pursuing a dream is harmful. I have interviewed too many thirty-somethings who never gave up on that "one thing," and now have no homes or families, and it's usually combined with a résumé in shambles, preventing them from capturing a career position with a salary sufficient to support a decent lifestyle and family.

◆ ◆ ◆

REPLACING THE LIE WITH TRUTH:

PURSUING A DREAM is a good thing. In fact, there is no way anyone's dream can come true unless they pursue it. Pursuing anything worthwhile is going to involve determination, resilience, and persistence in the face of adversity.

The fact of the matter is that there does come a point in time for the vast majority when they should stop pursuing the dream, pivot, and prioritize what they need to do as more important than what they want to do. That point in time is when pursuing the dream is costing too much in the way of personal relationships, family, and finances. The sayings "the only way to achieve your dreams is to have no backup plan" and "burn the ships so you have nowhere else to go" all sound good, but too often, they result in disaster. In fact, having no backup plan can result in success—but for every success there are countless disasters. Is that gamble really worth it? Here is what leaders should say about pursuing dreams:

> "Everyone has a true calling, a purpose for which they were born. Those who find a career which satisfies their true calling or purpose are very blessed/fortunate. Most people will eventually find their true calling, and their dream career can become a reality. It is simply a matter of time when that happens. Pursue your calling, your dream, with everything you have, but pivot or change direction when it begins to impact your relationships, family, or finances."

HALF-TRUTH #15:

"You are too valuable to us to allow you to leave. Effective immediately, we are making this right. In fact, we had planned on it before this meeting."

Cherish those who seek the truth but beware of those who find it.

—Voltaire

Neil McNulty (to the general manager of a large manufacturing plant): "This is an excellent position you are trying to fill. My company would be privileged to conduct the search to fill it. Why is it open?"

Plant General Manager: "It isn't open just yet, but it will be soon."

Neil McNulty: "Is the individual doing the job right now being promoted or moved?"

Plant General Manager: "Moved, but not promoted. As soon as I find his replacement, he is being moved all right, completely out of the company! He just resigned, and I had to buy him back to get him to stay. I don't take kindly to coercion."

◆ ◆ ◆

THIS FINAL HALF-TRUTH actually qualifies as a blatant lie for most managers who say it in response to the resignation of a key employee. When a key team member leaves, it can have devastating consequences for a company, and many business leaders will make promises they know they cannot keep due to the shock of the moment. That is a big reason why smart and ethical business leaders, as much as possible, will not allow any employee to hold so much power that if they left it would set the company back. These leaders structure the company to have at least two people in every key function, so they are not faced with big problems caused by one person's resignation. They also never attempt to buy back an employee who has resigned.

If in the industry long enough, all executive search consultants will eventually receive a confidential replacement search from a company. These assignments are often the result of someone resigning and the boss persuaded them to withdraw the resignation. The reality of a large hole that they (the boss) will need to plug is too much to deal with, so they say whatever it takes to keep the person around long enough to replace them.

To be fair, not all the bosses are lying when they

make promises in response to a resignation. Sometimes a boss sincerely intends to keep their word. Then, over time, the "buy back" weighs heavily on their minds and resentment builds toward the employee. Based upon my experience, usually at about six months after the withdrawn resignation, the business leader decides to terminate that employee. Or the employee starts contacting headhunters to get placed because they sense friction with their boss and realize the end is near. The reasons for the end of the employee-employer relationship vary, but usually it's because the boss feels they were the victim of strong-arm tactics, or they feel they can no longer completely trust the employee with sensitive company matters.

This half-truth (usually a blatant lie) is included in this book because it is probably the most common lie that employees fall victim to. If one has a thirty or forty-year career, they will probably work at several companies. It is very rare today for anyone to work at the same company for an entire career unless they are the owner of the business. That means they will need to leave one company to join another, and that also means resigning.

Changing employers is one of the most stressful life events according to mental health experts. That's mostly because a career is such a major part of someone's life, ranking with family and close friends. In fact, for many, their employment is how they define themselves. This is especially so with those who are in the middle years of their careers and have much invested both emotionally and financially. Accordingly, the stress of leaving one employer for another, like any major venture into the unknown, is great, because it involves risk.

When resigning from a company, most employees will be extremely nervous, stressed, and, frankly, vulnerable. Only the most unemotional people who can compartmentalize extremely well do not have second thoughts about changing employers, and even if they hate their jobs. The employers know this, and some are very skilled at pushing the right buttons to keep someone from leaving. Most often, remaining after resignation results in disaster for the employee. That disaster is usually unemployment—they are terminated and now have no job at all because they no longer have the position they resigned for.

The bottom line is this: someone should never remain at an employer from whom they have resigned, no matter what promises are made.

◆ ◆ ◆

REPLACING THE LIE WITH TRUTH:
WHEN A VALUABLE employee resigns from a well-respected company, it is not a positive reflection

on the company and the resigning person's supervisor. In response, some business leaders will say and do whatever is necessary to keep the employee from leaving. To that end, many are lying when they make promises to keep them on board. When the employee remains after withdrawing a resignation, it is extremely rare for them to receive a positive outcome down the road.

What can an employer say that is truthful yet might have a positive effect on retaining a departing key employee? Actually, there is nothing that should be attempted to keep the individual in the company. The outcomes for both company and employee rarely end well after a resigned employee remains in the company. The best path forward is a statement that is positive, similar to the following:

> "I wish you the best always, and you are always welcome here. Also, if I can assist you with references or anything else, let me know. After you get your feet on the ground in your new position, I hope you reconnect with me and let me know how things are going. Good luck, and I wish you great success in your new assignment."

THE TAKEAWAYS

◆ ◆ ◆

THIS BOOK PROBABLY required no more than an hour or two to read. It is intended as a quick reference to review from time to time, and especially when you hear a business leader tell one or more of the lies and half-truths discussed in this book. In fact, you will probably smile the next time you hear someone tell one. They might actually believe what they are saying, so technically they are not lying, and therefore be careful not to immediately judge them negatively. Before concluding that you are hearing a lie, always investigate and dig deeper. However, it is not a bad idea to remain skeptical when hearing or reading one or more of the business lies examined in this book.

This book might also have struck a nerve or two, creating laughter or perhaps even anger. This is particularly so if you are a business leader who occasionally tells one or more of the fifteen the lies and half-truths yourself. You might now need to explain or clarify your positions, especially if your employees read this book. Not to worry. The rephrasing at the end of each chapter can be helpful in delivering the same message in a truthful manner, and without looking as though you were lying all along in your previous statements.

The lies and half-truths discussed in this book are often well-intended and aspirational, but they remain mostly less than truthful, nonetheless. They can and should be rephrased for truth. Finally, this book is not an exposé. It is simply a resource for good—to spark an examination for truth in what is heard often, to accomplish what are often good intentions, and to make American business better.

Go out and seek truth. Share it when you find it.

ABOUT THE AUTHOR

◆ ◆ ◆

NEIL MCNULTY IS a leading national authority on employment and careers. He began his executive search and recruiting career in 1984 with Management Recruiters International (MRI/MRI Network), the USA's preeminent executive search and placement firm. At MRI, he completed hundreds of searches, from entry-level to C-suite, eventually leading three award-winning offices. He established long-term relationships with some of the world's finest companies, to include PepsiCo, Cintas, Kraft Foods, Perrier Group, Coca-Cola, Nabisco, Alcoa, and many others. Neil is also one of America's top experts on active-duty military members in career transition to civilian careers, and he is recognized by his industry as having placed into civilian careers more military veterans, one on one, than anyone else in America today. He founded MMG Leaders (MMGLeaders.com). With offices from Virginia to Washington state, it became the preeminent company in its sector of the staffing industry by using the proprietary geographically targeted placement model Neil created in 1986. Neil has also served as CEO or president of three large nonprofit organizations serving marginalized populations and healthcare. He speaks widely on career issues, delivering conference keynotes and commencement addresses at some of America's most prestigious colleges and universities. He has been quoted frequently in the national media and in bestselling books. Finally, and for which he is most proud, he is a retired US Marine Corps officer and resides with his family in southeastern Virginia.

www.ingramcontent.com/pod-product-compliance
Lightning Source LLC
LaVergne TN
LVHW041609070526
838199LV00052B/3059